Civil Society in Sri Lanka

Civil Society in Sri Lanka

New Circles of Power

Nira Wickramasinghe

Sage Publications
New Delhi ◇ Thousand Oaks ◇ London

Copyright © Nira Wickramasinghe, 2001

First published in 2001 by

Sage Publications India Pvt Ltd
M-32 Market, Greater Kailash-I
New Delhi-110 048

Sage Publications Inc
2455 Teller Road
Thousand Oaks, California 91320

Sage Publications Ltd
6 Bonhill Street
London EC2A 4PU

Published by Tejeshwar Singh for Sage Publications India Pvt Ltd, typeset in 10pt CentSchbook BT by SIVA Math Setters, Chennai, and printed at Chaman Enterprises, Delhi.

Library of Congress Cataloging-in-Publication Data

Wickramasinghe, Nira.
    Civil society in Sri Lanka: new circles of power/Nira Wickramasinghe.
      p. cm.
    Includes bibliographical references and index.
      1. Civil society--Sri Lanka. 2. Non-governmental organizations--Sri Lanka. 3. Economic assistance--Sri Lanka. 4. Humanitarian assistance--Sri Lanka. I. Title.

JQ659.A15 W53   300 .95493-dc21   2001   2001049199

ISBN: 0-7619-9576-5 (US-Hb)
         81-7829-004-9 (India-Hb)

Sage Production Team: Abantika Chatterji, Shweta Vachani,
                    O.P. Bhasin, and Santosh Rawat

For Maninda, Abhijit and Pratik

Contents

List of Abbreviations

ASEAN	Association of South East Asian Nations
CBO	Community-based organizations
CIDA	Canadian International Development Agency
EXCOM	Executive Committee of the High Commissioner's Program
ECOSOC	Economic and Social Council
FORUT	Norwegian acronym of Campaign for Development and Solidarity
GA	government agent
GP	Gami Puduwa (village re-awakening)
GPU	Gami Puduwa Upadeshaka
HNB	Hatton National Bank
IDPS	internally displaced persons
ICRC	International Committee of the Red Cross
IMF	International Monetary Fund
IPKF	Indian Peace Keeping Force
IRO	International Refugee Organization
JTF	Janasaviya Trust Fund
JVP	Janata Vimukti Peramuna
LDC	less developed country
LTTE	Liberation Tigers of Tamil Eelam
MOU	Memorandum of Understanding
MSF	Médecins sans Frontières
NGO	non-governmental organization
NIC	newly industrialized country
NORAD	Norwegian Agency for Development

NOVIB	Netherlands Organization for International Development Cooperation
NPI	new partnership initiative
ORCS	Open Relief Centers
OXFAM	Oxford Committee for Famine Relief
PSIDC	Public Sector Infrastructure Development Company
PTA	Prevention of Terrorism Act
QUANGO	Quasi Non-Governmental Organization
RAAFD	Research and Application for Alternative Financing for Development
SAARC	South Asian Association for Regional Cooperation
SAP	Structural Adjustment Policy
SEEDS	Sarvodaya Economic Enterprises Development Services
SIDA	Swedish International Development Agency
SLFP	Sri Lanka Freedom Party
UNHCR	United Nations High Commission for Refugees
UNP	United National Party
USAID	United States Agency for International Development
VSSO	Voluntary Service Organization
WHO	World Health Organization
WIDER	World Institute for Development Economic Research

Acknowledgements

I have incurred many debts in the writing of this book. The International Center for Ethnic Studies in Colombo, with which I have been associated for the past 11 years, gave me institutional support for revising the manuscript during a period of leave from the university. I am especially grateful to Radhika Coomaraswamy for providing valuable comments on the draft and to Mr P. Tambirajah for his assistance in all dealings with my publishers.

The idea of putting these essays together in a volume was given to me a few years ago by the late Dr Neelan Tiruchelvam. After reading an early version of the paper on partnership, he gently urged me to place more faith in civil society and society in general. This thought remained with me as I revised the papers.

I am grateful to all those friends and colleagues who played a part in the production of this book, including my fellow participants at conferences in Washington, Providence, Dacca, Hawali and Singapore, where these papers were first presented, and the several individuals who later read my drafts and offered constructive comments. Among them I must single out Muthiah Alagappa, Imtiaz Ahmed, Mortimer Sellers, Ifthekar Zaman and Marina Carter.

I am grateful to the following publishers and institutions for allowing me to use in this book sections from my previously published articles. Chapter 1 is reprinted with minor changes from *Asian Security Practice: Material and Ideational Influences*, edited by Muthiah Alagappa, with the permission of the publishers, Stanford University Press, Copyright 1998 by the Board of Trustees of the Lelani Stanford Junior University. Chapter 2 is reprinted from *The New World Order: Sovereignty, Human Rights and the Self-Determination of Peoples* (Oxford, Washington DC, Berg, 1996) edited by Mortimer Sellers with the permission of the publishers. The research for Chapter 3 was funded by the World Bank's Robert S. McNamara Fellowships Program 'as part of its mission to encourage the leadership potential of young researchers, and to facilitate empirical research on issues critical to improving the lives of the most vulnerable in the developing world'. Chapter 4 is a revised version of 'Humanitarian Relief Organizations in Times of War and Challenges to Sovereignty; The Case of Sri Lanka', *RCSS Policy Studies 1, 1997*, with the permission of the Regional Centre for Strategic Studies.

Last but not least I would like to express my heartfelt thanks to my parents who nurtured me, and to my family for supporting me and providing a continual source of joy during the preparation of this work.

Introduction

Most developing states are, in varying degrees of intensity, participating in a growing process of integration of their national economies into a global world economy. Factors of production have become increasingly mobile as capital moves freely and technology and information diffuse almost instantly across national boundaries. Certain global trends are often highlighted as characterizing the 1990s. Interdependence among societies existed before, but what is new is the erasing of costs of communicating over distance as a result of the information revolution. The character of the nation-state too is believed to be mutating as the workings of the global economy undermine the sovereignty of national governments. Analysts have predicted the end of the nation-state and even the end of geography (Omae, 1995). New forms of allegiance are believed to be emerging which seek forms of organization beyond national sovereignty. The recent growth of regional groupings in Asia modeled on the Association of South East Asian Nations or ASEAN is a case in point. The metaphor of globalization is nevertheless too general to evoke the subtleties of the changing relations between states and international regimes of culture, politics and economics of the late 1990s. Globalization as a process encompasses such a vast arena that its usage just as that of the concept of modernization in the 1960s often ceases to explain anything. Arjun Appadurai highlights two meanings to the word 'globalization': first as a socio-economic formation and second as a term of folk ideology in journalism and in the corporate world. In both senses, it marks a set of transitions in the global political economy since the 1970s. He argues that during the next decades, multinational forms of capitalist organization began to be replaced by transnational, flexible and irregular forms of organization. Labor, finance, technology and technological capital began to be assembled in ways that treated national boundaries as mere constraints or fictions (Appadurai, 1998: 5).

The new world order that emerged in the 1970s and deployed its wings to touch the entire globe is perhaps better described in the Hegelian term of 'circle of circles' each delineating areas of sovereignty or power. That the world is today interconnected in so many ways is obvious to any observer. The different forces and processes that induce this connectiveness are, however, best looked at separately rather than encompassed in the framework of a shibboleth-like term such as globalization. This book has been compiled with this purpose in mind.

The four essays in this volume, written in the mid and late 1990s, address in different ways some of the new international and transnational forces that are shaping the developmental state in Sri Lanka. These new circles of power that are being drawn by international financial organizations, humanitarian relief organizations, and northern NGOs are not only reorganizing the political economy of the country, but through the creation of transnational networks integrating it into a new cultural and ideological world order. The context in which these forces are deployed is a changing one: in the early 1990s the mood was for openness to the international market, the harnessing of foreign investment and trade in concert with new technologies. Today, the economic crisis that has swept through many of the economies of Asia calls for some rethinking of the benefits of following the 'Washington consensus' in favor of free markets, trade and investment.

While the emergence of a civil society in Sri Lanka has been discussed in numerous works of scholars and practitioners, its incorporation into a global network has rarely been investigated. The rise of an 'international', 'global' or 'world civil society' including NGOs as well as networks of scholars, religious and other voluntary organizations, research institutes and media collectives is leading to a redefinition of the compass between state and society. This 'world civil society' supports and harnesses values such as human rights in a form that tends to challenge the primacy of the state. But its liberal critique of the state sometimes leads its constituents to be coopted by global financial institutions that harbor a similar mistrust of the state. Another cause for worry is the progressive breakdown in communication between the increasingly global and extraterritorial elites and the ever more 'localized' rest.

This volume does not purport, however, to trace the emergence, development and role of a global civil society networking in Sri Lanka but rather it focuses on particular occurrences where global civil society impinges on the way security, sovereignty, development, governance are perceived and conceptualized.

Security issues today dominate the making of foreign and internal policy in a country such as Sri Lanka that has been in a state of war since the late 1970s when Tamil militancy took up arms against the state. The state rhetoric was for long primarily about national security, that is protection of the boundaries of the sovereign state of Sri Lanka from encroachments, first on the part of India, then by unlawful sons of the soil. The core values to be protected were territorial integrity and political independence. The first essay in this volume analyzes the local NGO network and human rights organizations as forming a new circle of power that challenges and contests the state conception of security in contemporary Sri Lanka. Rather than focusing on the nation-state, these forces emphasize people's security and the security of the community from threats that often come from the state apparatus—armed forces, political parties or from 'globalization'.

Donor countries increasingly link development aid to human rights and other political and moral considerations. The second chapter recognizes the importance of human rights but questions the recent emergence of 'good governance' as a decisive factor in aid policy and development assistance. Nations subscribing to the International Covenant on Civil and Political Rights or to the International Covenant on Economic, Social and Cultural Rights agree, in effect, to cede part of their sovereignty to world institutions. But the World Bank is attempting to forge a New World Order where there will be governance without government. In this technicist and single-track approach governments would still operate and still be sovereign in a number of ways, but some of their authority would be relocated towards subnational collectivities. This chapter highlights the need for development programs that are more mindful of the social, cultural and political consequences of their intervention.

The third chapter addresses the concept of partnership in development that has to a large extent replaced aid in the development discourse in Sri Lanka. Partnership is increasingly invoked by multilateral donor agencies. In their ideal vision, harmonious relations exist between the state, the private sector and the NGO community all engaged in 'developing' their society into a liberal democratic one under the watchful eye of the donor. The 1990s have witnessed a drive of development from the simple goals of poverty alleviation to holistic aims of redesigning the state and society of the country. Partnership is no longer a concept linking donor and receiver but rather linking between them, all the different components of the society which receives assistance. This vision emphasizes the role of NGOs in the development of the country. In so doing donors are making sure that the constituency, which initially refused structural adjustment programs collaborates and that social order prevails.

The second and third chapters in this volume examine the circles of dependence created through an aid and developmental regime. They suggest that the Sri Lankan developing state is not only redefining its course in conceptual terms invented and imposed by the agencies—governance, participation, partnership are examples of the grid according to which minds are asked to rethink their condition—it is also expected to follow, without ushering any protest, the guidance of the international financial bodies and funders in general with regard to what in reality constitutes development. The reason being, that as many modern states and governments, Sri Lanka's state has grounded its legitimacy in significant measure on its ability to effect development.

The fourth chapter analyzes the relation between humanitarianism in Sri Lanka and state sovereignty reading autobiographies of three relief organizations: International Committee of the Red Cross, United Nations High Commission for Refugees (UNHCR) and Médecins sans Frontières (MSF).

This chapter argues that the formation of a global civil society founded on an allegiance to human rights, which transcends state sovereignty and claims an ideological and territorial (i.e., boundary zones) domain for itself, does not actually constitute a denial of sovereignty as a concept. What these postnational formations are moving towards is a share of sovereignty and the constitution of rival sovereignties. As Appadurai writes:

> It is a heady moment full of great creativity and uncertainty. Many proposals are circulating for new kinds of public spheres, third spaces, virtual communities, transnations, and diasporic networks.... The failure of nation-states to produce convincing fantasies of the commensurability of its citizens ('the people') compels some to imagine recombinant forms of non-territorial, life world sovereignties, while it forces others into even more primordial and violent affiliations of territory, religion and race (Appadurai, 1998).

Reading these lines, the metaphor of 'circle of circles' delineating power and sovereignties seems already passé for the new millennium. Other words will have to be coined to capture the dimensions of space, time, myth and imagination in the global struggle for economic and cultural power of the future.

References

Appadurai, Arjun. 1998. 'Dead Certainty: Ethnic Violence in the Era of Globalization', *Eighth Punitham Tiruchelvam Memorial Lecture*, 31 January 1998, p. 5. Colombo: ICES.

Omae, Kenichi. 1995. *The End of the Nation-state*. New York: The Free Press.

Chapter 1

The Many Faces of Security in Sri Lanka

If we have to live as minorities, we might as well live in a place that promises security to the children (Kamala, a victim of the 1983 riots).

Over two hundred thousand people have been liberated by the security forces. Over one thousand families have been cleared so far by the security forces to return to Vallikaman division. Security forces captured a van transporting terrorists. All terrorists were killed on the spot (Government communique, Operation Riviresa II, April 1996).

Among the multiplicity of voices speaking about national security there are some that challenge or even contest the state's conception of security.[1] Security, it appears, is not a static phenomenon but a changing, wavering perception. Borrowing from Ashis Nandy's formulation, I would liken it to an 'amoeba' word that can take any shape and convey any meaning (Nandy, 1994: 1). This chapter starts with the premise that security per se does not exist. There are only *conceptions* of security—and hence of national security—that vary from agent to agent, from consciousness to consciousness, along lines of community, class, and gender, and over time. Conceptions of security can be understood only in the context of the discourse, conventions of argument, habits, customs, and political actions that produce them.

Thus my focus is both on national security as it has been defined by the state at different periods and on the challenges put forward by groups that contest the state's definition. Above all, I wish to address perceptions or narratives of security that are not usually given a voice in academic studies. Although marginalized, such perceptions inform the consciousness of many Sri Lankans. But do these muted voices count? To what extent do they pose a challenge to the state's perception of security? Do they in any way influence power sufficiently to form new circles of power?

In Sri Lanka, it is possible to distinguish at least three different conceptions of state security. The first is the state's definition of security as national security, a conception rooted in the notion of territoriality and infused with the idea that the security of the whole equals the security of its components. In this view, the primary threat to security is external. This conception has dominated state thinking and behavior since independence. Since the Janata Vimukti Peramuna (JVP) insurrection in 1971 and the wars in the north and east in the 1980s, however, internal concerns have begun to dominate. This second notion of state security, with its emphasis on internal threats, is now being displaced at the state level, under the government of Chandrika Bandaranaike Kumaratunge, by a third conception. The government, which has close links with human rights groups and the non-governmental sector on the whole, has proposed a concept of national security that encompasses human values as well. The limitations of this third conception of security, however, are evidenced by the violent secessionist challenge the state faces from the Liberation Tigers of Tamil Eelam (LTTE) and the military option it has been compelled to adopt after the collapse of negotiations between the state and the LTTE.

The first part of this chapter examines the state's three conceptions of national security. The second investigates the non-governmental approach to security as human security and its impact on the state approach. The final part examines challenges to the state and non-governmental conceptions of security that stem from anti-systemic groups such as the Janata Vimukti Peramuna, which on two occasions has tried through violent means to capture power, and also from the Buddhist Sangha (order of Buddhist monks).

National Security as State Security: Evolution from External to Internal Considerations

For the person on the street, security has many meanings from 'safety as in job security' to 'the country and the people living free of troubles'.[2] In a way, these meanings reflect the perception of many scholars today who concede that security is not confined to military security, which can be defined as the absence of threat or conflict. Security does have its intrinsic positive elements—presence of values, satisfaction of needs, a sense of feeling secure and striving unhindered for growth and development—but the concept also implies subtle threats to economic, social, and cultural independence. Until recently, however, academics and diplomats in Sri Lanka rarely accepted a maximalist definition of security such as that of James N. Rosenau, who defines security both in the personal sense of securing a meaningful identity and in the collective sense of maintaining territorial integrity, political stability, and economic well-being (Rosenau, 1994: 255–81). When speaking of security, state officials and international relations specialists still tend to focus on the security of the state. Let us begin by examining the state discourse on security, which is mirrored in mainstream academic writings on security, while noting that the understanding of security has changed over the years. Since independence it is fairly safe to say that the state rhetoric of security in Sri Lanka has been primarily about national security rather than people's security. Like most rhetoric encouraged by the state and the major mass media, the language of national security is not innocent. The noble cause of safeguarding the nation is used to confer legitimacy on other, perhaps less noble, causes and acts.

To analyze the state's conceptions of security one has to rely, if cautiously, on selected documents of the state, such as the speeches of officials, to get at the dynamics below the surface. One must also be aware that those officials do not usually base their actions on carefully formulated sets of objectives. Many government transactions are unplanned; important decisions are often made in response to urgent pressures rather than as part of a coherent and far-sighted policy. It is also useful to distinguish between the 'declaratory' and the 'operational' objectives of policy-makers. Official definitions of security lean toward a realist approach that is, security is defined primarily from the military strategic perspective and the focus is on protecting the state from physical attacks from within and without. The object of national security is to preserve the state or, in Aristotelian terms, to achieve 'the good for the state'. In this sense the good of the individual is considered secondary by Sri Lanka's policy-makers, who indeed could have cited Aristotle: 'Though it is worthwhile to attain the end merely for one man, it is finer and more godlike to attain it for a nation or for city-states' (Sen, 1990: 4). But again, is it correct to speak of a state approach without differentiating between the governments that have ruled the country since independence? How did the state's policy-makers understand security in the 1950s and 1960s? Did they actually think in the same terms?

The Foreign Policy Approach: External Threats to Security

My purpose here is not to give a chronological account of the security problems during a certain period but to show how the framework of discourse has shifted from the external to the internal. According to mainstream thinking, both official and academic, the major security problems for most of the countries in South Asia have to do with their relationship with India. As Shelton U. Kodikara has observed, the 'security dilemma' that confronts the South Asian states arises from the fact that the region is militarily Indo-centric. The fundamental security problem, he says, is one in which the states peripheral to India seek a maximization of security vis-à-vis India while India itself seeks to regionalize security within a subcontinental framework (Kodikara, 1993: 8). Most studies of Sri Lanka's security adopt a regional outlook: Sri Lanka can be understood only as part of South Asia or the world system.

Gamini Keerawella stresses that fear of 'Big Brother' was one of the main elements of the defense-oriented perspective of the first United National Party (UNP) government of 1948–56. Even in the 1970s during Sirimavo Bandaranaike's premiership, Indo-Sri Lankan relations were characterized by suspicion. The demarcation of the maritime boundary between the two countries in the Palk Strait and the Gulf of Mannar was a high priority (Keerawella, 1990: 180). In the 1970s and 1980s, the development of the Indian Ocean as a zone of peace was perceived as central to Sri Lanka's security. The conference on the Indian Ocean due to be held in 1981 never materialized, however, and the UN Declaration of the Indian Ocean as a peace zone has yet to be implemented (Kodikara, 1993). Thus in the state's conception, Sri Lanka's security could be maintained by a sort of cordon sanitaire wrapped around its coastline. In the writings of Sri Lankan analysts, one finds that the notion of a secure boundary and territorial protection is at the core of the state's appreciation of security. The regime in power is irrelevant. Thus, for all intents and purposes, security is equated with national security whether in the language of diplomats or mainstream academics. Until the mid-1950s, threats to national security were perceived as coming from outside.

After the emergence of a militant Tamil separatist movement in Sri Lanka, the state's apprehension sharpened and was long focused on the possibility of Indian military intervention in support of Tamil militants in the northern province. The state has what is often called a minority complex vis-à-vis the subcontinent, where 65 million Tamils live. Not only has Sri Lanka never integrated with the mainland economies on the subcontinent, it has, in fact, made overtures for membership in the Association of Southeast Asian Nations (ASEAN) in 1981 and 1984. This policy was guided by Colombo's interest in attracting ASEAN capital to the free industrial zones under preferential terms. But security too played an important part. Sri Lanka was interested in obtaining support from the informal ASEAN security system because of its apprehension over the external threat posed by the possibility of Indian intervention. Due to these preoccupations, Colombo's commitment to the South Asian Association for Regional Cooperation (SAARC) was somewhat questionable at the outset. It was during the UNP era, in 1987, that an Indian peacekeeping force landed in the northeast of Sri Lanka to disarm the Tamil militants—thus, in the common perception, threatening the sovereignty of the state of Sri Lanka. Not surprisingly, after this event, the fear of an Indian invasion of the island and of Indian interference in the general affairs of the country remained the central security issue. But the 1987 intervention by the Indian peacekeeping force also broke the psychological barrier. The Indians had indeed come, but they left in 1989. P.R. Chari questions the Indian hegemony thesis. First, he argues, the approach ignores the superpower's role in exacerbating subcontinental tensions. And second, it ignores sub-regional tensions (Chari, 1987: 50–60). In the case of the Tamil militant movement in Sri Lanka, it is obvious that ethnopolitical issues spilled across national boundaries.

Violence and the Internal Dimension

Two events led to a change in the state's perception of security as a predominantly external concern. The first was the JVP revolt in 1971. The second was the escalation of the armed struggle of the LTTE in the northern and eastern provinces in the early 1980s.

The Janata Vimukti Peramuna Insurrections: Security as Order

In 1971, the JVP, a violent political movement, tried to topple the leftist government of Sirimavo Bandaranaike but failed. It resumed the effort in the late 1980s in an even more violent manner using murder, torture, and intimidation. The trigger for this resurgence was the 1987 Indo-Sri Lankan Accord, which sanctioned the use of Indian troops in Sri Lanka to quell the LTTE in the north and east. The JVP movement nearly succeeded in destroying the state institutions but was crushed by the Sri Lankan security forces working with death squads.

In social and ideological terms, the JVP is made up of radical Sinhalese Buddhists who are both anti-Tamil and anti-Indian. Many of its members are political and social reformers drawn from the educated unemployed youth of the south. In 1971, the JVP sought to 'save' the country from eastern imperialism and Indian expansionist designs. In 1987–89, it again sought to 'save' the country from an unholy trinity of American imperialism, Indian imperialism, and Tamil expansionism. The JVP became a security issue: for the first time the state had to face serious internal threats. The JVP insurrection was first ana- lyzed by state officials and mainstream academics as an anti- state movement that would have to be crushed by the security forces to safeguard the legitimate state. There is at the core of Sri Lanka's state ideology the notion of its responsibility to ensure a *dharmista samajaya*, a just society. The state and its security forces see the *'dharmista* society' as one where social justice prevails but can be achieved only through political stabil- ity. The ruler and his agents undertake to govern righteously, to provide for all citizens according to their merits and virtues, and to bring about material benefits for the ruled. In return, the ruled are expected to accept the status quo and to confine their dissent within the bounds of the political order. Crushing the JVP insurrection was, therefore, a security imperative that the state and the security forces took upon themselves.

In 1971 and 1988–89, national security was not all-inclusive: it meant, in effect, protecting the legitimacy of the ruling classes, which were threatened by a political revolt of disad- vantaged youth who were attempting to capture state power. The JVP's activities were described in the state media as sub- versive threats to the state that could be dealt with only through the use of the Public Security Act. In 1971, when offi- cials defined the political threat posed by the insurgents as a security problem, security was understood as 'order' or as preservation of the status quo. There were plans to 'tighten security all over Ceylon', and Mrs Bandaranaike proclaimed she was 'ready for any threat to the peace' (*Daily News*, 6–7 March 1971).

Although the 1971 insurrection and the JVP's resurgence in the 1980s were explained by officials as a security threat to the state, and thereby used as a rationale for the state's authori- tarian tendencies, those two events were not described as secur- ity problems by political analysts until the late 1980s. In political science, works dealing with developments in Sri Lanka and in specific studies of the JVP where, interestingly, the term *security* is invisible[3], the analytical framework was different. It is only since the late 1980s, and in studies specifically pertain- ing to security, that the concept of security is used to analyze political threats from within such as the JVP (Werake and

Jayasekera, 1995). It is no coincidence that the inclusion of security as an analytical concept to appraise internal threats to the state was adopted at the time Tamil militancy began to pose a serious threat to the state.

Ethnic Conflict and Security of the South

The ethnic conflict became a security problem for the state only in the 1980s when the Sri Lankan police and military were incapable of suppressing the increasingly violent LTTE struggle in the northern and eastern provinces and Colombo was under threat from terrorist attacks and bombs. When the ethnic conflict began to affect the majority community, it became a security issue.

The Sri Lanka Tamils—or Ceylon Tamils, as they were called until the 1970s—constitute 12.6 per cent of the total population; the Up-country Tamils, whose antecedents were brought from southern India by the British in the nineteenth century to work as laborers in the new plantation sector, constitute 5.5 per cent. The Sri Lanka Tamils live not only in the northern and eastern parts of the island—the areas militants refer to as the Tamil homelands—but also in the south, whereas the Up-country Tamils live in the central highlands where the tea plantations are located.

The demand for a separate state for the Tamil people arose from the failure of repeated attempts to meet Sri Lanka Tamil aspirations. This failure, together with growing economic problems and rising unemployment, contributed to the rise of assertive and aggressive Tamil militancy.

There was a difference in degree between the non-violent methods used by the Federal Party and the Tamil United Liberation Front to push for their separatist demands and the later use of terrorist methods, particularly suicide bombers, against civilians in the south by the LTTE. There was first a 'communal problem'. At the time of independence, the Ceylon Tamils held a disproportionately high number of jobs in the prestigious Ceylon Civil Service and places in the most important higher education faculties (Wickramasinghe, 1995). To combat the advantages enjoyed by Tamils after independence, the Sinhalese majority adopted two policies that are the source of much of the subsequent discontent of the Tamils: a 'Sinhala only' language policy and a quota system based on race and residence (referred to as 'standardization') for admission to university. When the Sinhala Only Act was adopted in 1956, a proposal to include a clause on the use of Tamil was dropped because of pressure from extremist Buddhist groups. Tamil protests led in 1956 to the Bandaranaike-Chelvanayakam Pact, which provided for the use of Tamil in Tamil areas and would have established regional councils with powers to enact agriculture, education, and colonization schemes. The pact was never implemented—again because of strong objections by Buddhist elements—and in 1958 the first major outbreak of communal violence occurred.

In the 1950s with the resurgence of Sinhalese nationalism and the emergence of the Federal Party, which pressed for a Tamil homeland, officials came to look upon national security not only as an interstate problem but also as an internal issue: protecting the unity of the state. 'We must find a formula to preserve the unity and maintain the unity of Ceylon,' said S. Corea, minister of commerce, trade, and fisheries, to his Chilaw electorate in 1956 (*Ceylon Daily News*, 9 January 1956). The term *security*, however, was still not commonly coupled with *internal*. The crisis facing the country in the mid-1950s was described as a communal problem rather than a security issue.

In 1958, a rumor that a Tamil had killed a Sinhalese sparked off nationwide communal riots. Hundreds of people, mostly Tamils, died. A dusk-to-dawn curfew was declared throughout the country, press censorship was enforced, and the Federal Party was banned. The Governor General, Sir Oliver Goonetilleke, declared a state of emergency on the island 'in the interests of public security, the preservation of public order, and the maintenance of supplies and services essential to the life of the community' (*Ceylon Daily News*, 26 May 1958; *Silumina*, 25 May 1958). After 1958, national security took on a wider meaning that encompassed not only preserving the integrity and unity of the state but also protecting the people. Security of the people gradually began to mean security of the majority community, the southern people who faced threats from aliens.

A watershed in the 'Sinhalization' of the state came in May 1972 with the passage of the republican constitution, which asserted Sinhalese Buddhist cultural forms and contained weaker protection for minorities. For many Tamils, the 1972 constitutional provisions on religion and language confirmed their feeling of being second-class citizens. Their sense of alienation was further reinforced by the United Front government's policies on university entrance, which brought down dramatically the proportion of Tamils entering the university.

The Tamil response was first civil disobedience and then separatism. In 1976, the Tamil United Liberation Front demanded the formation of a separate state of Tamil Eelam in the areas that were considered the Tamil homelands in the north and east. Those areas accounted for two-thirds of the coastline and one-third of the country. This demand paved the way for militants, who began by assassinating Tamils associated with the ruling party and then started attacking state targets (Nissan, 1996).

Tensions between Tamils and Sinhalese increased during the Sri Lanka Freedom Party (SLFP) rule of Mrs Bandaranaike, and a major outbreak of violence occurred in August 1977, only a few months after the election of the Jayawardene-led United National Party (UNP) government. The third major outbreak of communal violence occurred in August 1981. Mutual fear and anger had developed as terrorist attacks against police in the north increased, accompanied by the detention of Tamil youths incommunicado and by arson and looting by police in Jaffna. Their burning of the Jaffna Public Library, a Tamil cultural center, was particularly resented and is still referred to as an early example of the lawlessness of the security forces.

Once the LTTE began to retaliate by sending suicide squads to the capital to destroy army or business establishments—in the process killing civilians in the south—the state's definition of security gained a further complexity. The new understanding privileges the security of the south, because its institutions and people are under threat from terrorist attacks. Although national security has assumed a new dimension—the security of the south is now given higher priority than that of any other region—the notion of territorial integrity remains at the core. Every night, the state television news broadcast updates the 'security situation' by giving a head count of the number of soldiers and terrorists killed in the northeast, an account of any terrorist attack perpetrated in the south, and measures taken to ensure the safety of the capital. The emphasis, however, is on the square footage of territory captured by the army in its various operations, not on the lives and deaths of human beings.

For the Sri Lankan state, internal security still entails protecting the boundaries of the state against secessionist movements—thus avoiding the dilution of state sovereignty and safeguarding it from external intervention. The notion of territoriality, therefore, still predominates in the state's perception of security. The concept of territory is crucial, too, in the state's understanding of nationalism and the nation-state. A nation-state is perceived as a spatial unit lying between borders that it must defend. Territory, as Louis Dumont defines it, is a continuous tract of country that symbolizes the unity of individuals who own parts of the country. If the nation is 'a collection of individuals and their properties', territory is the total of the properties belonging to that collection of individuals, known as the nation (Dumont, 1970: 108). Writing about the Indo-Sri Lankan Accord of 1987, Jayadeva Uyangoda points out that the primary aspect of the crisis was the prospect of territorial break-up and the disintegration of the Sri Lankan state. The theoretical possibility of a territorial split gained momentum with the outbreak of violence in the north and east and with the Tamil guerrilla campaigns (Uyangoda, 1989).

A certain consensus seems to have emerged on the necessity of military action against the LTTE. In the view of the UNP government in the early 1990s, only a military takeover of the north and the east could assure the security of the south. For the UNP, now in the opposition, military action has been found to be the only option. While he was prime minister, Ranil Wickremesinghe said, 'In the absence of any other option at the moment, security forces would continue their efforts to bring more areas in the North under the government's control' (*Hindu*, 11 March 1994). The government of Chandrika Bandaranaike Kumaratunge eventually adopted the military option because everything else had failed. She initiated a peace process, but after about four months of ceasefire the LTTE broke the truce by destroying two navy boats and firing heat-seeking missiles at two aircraft. The LTTE has subsequently tried to explain its breaking of the truce. It claims that the stance of the government expressed in the president's letter to the LTTE leader, Vellupillai Prabakharan, was that 'enough concessions and privileges had already been given to the Tamils and that further giving of anything would endanger the national security' (*The Island*, 23 April 1995). By April 1996 the government forces had recaptured the Jaffna peninsula, pushed the Tigers into the jungles of the Wanni, and given protection to its civilian population, which had been reduced to the status of refugees in LTTE-controlled areas. There are signs that the state is evolving a concept of security that combines security of the south from terrorist attacks, security of the north from guerrilla/military clashes, and protection of the sacrosanct boundaries of the nation-state from secessionist tendencies.

The State and Violence: From Army to Security Forces

Anthony Giddens has defined the nation-state as 'a set of institutional forms of governance maintaining an administrative monopoly over a territory with demarcated boundaries (borders), its rule being sanctioned by law and direct control of the means of internal and external violence' (Giddens, 1985: 121). He points out that a feature of the nation-state is its monopoly of the means of violence. Sri Lanka's situation demonstrates that when other groups in society—armed groups or insurgent movements— threaten that monopoly, the state is compelled to strengthen the instruments of internal pacification by transforming its army into a modern and technically advanced outfit that it calls its 'security forces'. The army played a ceremonial role during the first decades of independence and functioned in a limited capacity in assisting the police force to maintain law and order. The term then in vogue was 'law and order', which paradoxically has a much more authoritarian resonance than 'security'. It is as though, at some point, a reversal of meanings took place. During the decades of relative 'law and order' (1947 to the early 1980s), the political culture of the state and the army—whose officer corps was recruited from the upper classes and trained at Sandhurst—was above all democratic. Since the end of the 1970s, when Tamil groups took arms against the state, the Sri Lankan army has had to face real war for the first time.

The term *security* entered the vocabulary of the state at the end of this era of innocence—as though the predictable excesses of the armed forces would need to be semantically exorcized by use of the word *security*, which connotes protection and comfort rather than violence. *Security* and *forces* were thus coupled in an oxymoronic fashion. The 'internal security of the state' became a familiar phrase in the political jargon of the 1980s, and the army was rebaptized as the 'security forces'. It was a less confrontational way of making civil society accept the realities of war and violence under the guise of a discourse on 'security'.

The worsening of the ethnic conflict and the consequent expansion of the armed forces in the 1980s contributed to the creation of a 'security'-oriented state. The process of militarization and the special role assigned to the security forces resulted in several changes in the structure of the state, which in the last decade, according to some analysts, has begun to slide toward political authoritarianism (Warnapala, 1994). As Michel Foucault reminds us, 'politics has been conceived as a continuation, if not exactly and directly of war, at least of the military model as a fundamental means of preventing civil disorder'. What he suggests, in fact, is that politics, as a technique of internal peace and order, attempts to implement the mechanism of the perfect army and to a certain extent succeeds in training people to be disciplined and docile bodies (Rabinow, 1984: 185). The militarization of the state in the 1980s even influenced many Sri Lankans into uncritical admiration for a ruler such as Singapore's Lee Kuan Yew. It is not uncommon to hear people openly aver that what the country needs is 10 years of military rule, proper discipline, or a benevolent dictatorship.

The late 1970s and 1980s were a period of torture and deaths in custody, extrajudicial killings, and reprisal massacres. Arbitrary arrests and detention for long periods were common. Except for a period of five months, Sri Lanka has been in a state of emergency since 1983. In 1994, the left-of-center government of Chandrika Kumaratunge lifted the emergency decree in the south. In the north and the east, the security forces are still invested with extraordinary powers under the emergency regulations and the Prevention of Terrorism Act (PTA).[4] Indeed, since the outbreak of civil war, the security forces have been invested by the state with a sort of semi-divine aura. Under the UNP government it was considered a crime against the state to criticize the security forces even if they had committed excesses. The UNP manifesto of the 1994 elections offered a eulogy of the armed forces:

> Sri Lanka is proud of the heroism and dedication of its Security Forces. Despite being involved in violent and painful conflict with terrorism, our Security Forces have performed magnificently and with courage against every threat. Whereas increasing militarization in many countries brings about public hatred and contempt for their security forces, we have widespread sympathy and affection for the men and women who serve their motherland in our army, navy, airforce, and police (UNP Manifesto, *The Island*, 8 August 1984; ICES Election Literature Collection).

The security forces were the protectors of 'national security', modern-day heroes who fought courageously for the good of the country, the motherland. This feeling, encouraged by the state, seeped down to the Sinhalese people. Indeed, their widespread sympathy for the security forces was obvious during the late 1980s when the leftist and violence-prone JVP was gaining much ground among the poorer classes. The JVP's crucial mistake was to threaten the families of the security forces in its struggle against the state. That policy led to a major reversal in sympathy that helped the government to crush the JVP militarily. Initially, the Chandrika Kumaratunge government was ambivalent about the security forces. Although it started a campaign to bring to justice some of the military men involved in massacres, this effort has recently slowed. With the recent capture of Jaffna city, despite the obvious instances of violence, bribery, and corruption in the higher command, the security forces are once again hailed as the saviors of the nation.

Despite the changes in the state's conception of security, in the mainstream view security means protection of the boundaries of the sovereign state of Sri Lanka from encroachments—first on the part of India, then by unlawful sons of the soil. Very few studies offer an epistemological reflection on security. Security itself is a given. The core values to be protected are territorial integrity and political independence.

The only shift in emphasis in Sri Lanka has been that national security in recent years has come to mean, more and more, defending the sovereignty of the state against enemies from within.

Human Security: The Non-governmental Approach

Among members of majority and minority communities alike there is a sense that the state is incapable of ensuring their security. In the minds of the Sinhalese people, terrorist acts of the LTTE constitute the main threat to their own security and that of the country.[5] The fear is amplified by an impression of the state's helplessness. In November 1995, for example, all schools were closed for two months after the LTTE threatened to target school children. Eventually it was the Central Bank of Sri Lanka, in the heart of the business district of Colombo, that was blown to pieces in January 1996 by a suicide bomber, causing nearly 100 deaths and millions of rupees worth of damages.

For the minority community, the threat comes from the state institutions. Tamil civilians are frequently detained indiscriminately after guerrilla or terrorist attacks or during army operations. 'Security', according to a female Tamil undergraduate, 'is when you feel protected by the law. Security means protection of life. As a Tamil in the present day, the biggest threat is the security forces—having to produce identification.' Her words summarize the perception of the members of the Tamil community who were interviewed for this study. Unlike most Sinhalese, who when asked to define security said it meant to live 'without problem', Tamil men and women had a very precise understanding of the concept. The state's failure to protect all its citizens was highlighted. 'Being a Tamil, my name, my birthplace, is a source of suspicion. I am not accepted as a citizen of Sri Lanka. I don't have the same freedom as a man from the majority community', complained a Tamil teacher.[6]

Most people's conceptions of security share an important feature with the state's conception: both give a primary rank to the notion of territory. For the state, we noted that security is attached to the land and protection of the land or nation-state. For most individuals, the home constitutes the last bastion of security once the state fails its citizens. The events that took place in 1983 in Sri Lanka put the entire issue in perspective. After the deaths of 13 soldiers in Jaffna, the center of the separatist struggle, anti-Tamil riots broke out in Colombo. The mob targeted all Tamils. In this situation the recognized institutions of the state—the police and the armed forces whose duty it was to help the victims and control the violence—were seen as manifestly failing to do their duty, whereas the Christian Church offered help and sympathy. For the victims it was the informal network of friends and neighbors and the Christian Church organizations that provided the means for reformulating their lives. It is not surprising, then, that they should have felt betrayed by the state. The circle of security, therefore, has become smaller. As Kamala, a victim of the violence, recalls: 'I could not stand outside exposed to the violence. So I took my family and ran into the house. I suppose at that moment instinct makes us run into the security of our home' (Kanapatipillai, 1990: 344). For many victims, not even the home was secure.

Thus when the state breaks its contract to protect all its citizens, people are left to create their own security. For many in Sri Lanka this meant leaving the country altogether. Kamala's family felt that the future of Sri Lanka had no place for them and decided to migrate to New Zealand: 'If we have to live as minorities', she said, 'we might as well live in a place that promises security to the children' (ibid.: 334). Security means life.

Thus the individual's security is very much contingent on events. In the space of a few hours the state had changed its role from purveyor of security to prime threat and even oppressor. Another feature of individual security is that it is precisely when their security is threatened (by a bomb blast or riot) that people consciously reflect on their security needs. In situations of violence, therefore, security is not only contextual and malleable, it is also fundamentally reactive. Moreover, the feeling of threat persists. Many victims of violence, uprooted in different countries and more than 10 years after the events, still see crowds as hostile mobs. Former residents of Jaffna now in London or Toronto, who for years lived in fear of aerial bombing, still listen with apprehension to the sound of planes or helicopters. As Valli Kanapatipillai puts it, 'The violence did not just "erupt" and then disappear. Perhaps the difference between the threats from natural disasters, and violence coming from human agencies, is that the latter is experienced as continuous violence. It is not contained in time; like waves created by throwing a stone in the river, it has repercussions which far exceed the moment of its occurrence' (ibid.: 334).

Security as a Human Value

In 1994, the UNP lost the elections to the People's Alliance, a conglomeration of left, left-of-center, and minority parties. In contrast to previous governments for which security was mainly envisioned as national security, the present government's definition encompasses human values, too, at least at the declaratory level.

The election manifesto of the People's Alliance in the parliamentary elections of 1994 contained in its very title a notion of security at variance with the UNP approach: 'For a secure prosperous society where human values reign, devoid of corruption and terror.' In this formulation, it is society and not the state that has to be secure. Compared to the previous government, the emphasis had shifted from the state and a dominant concern for national security to a focus on civil society. In the manifesto, the three main aims of the People's Alliance underlined a 'liberal democratic' approach to rights and suggested the vital national values that must be protected: freedom to live in a humane society; a free and democratic society with law and order; and rapid and sustainable economic development (Gooneratne and Karunaratne, 1994). After the People's Alliance captured power and formed a government, its leader, Chandrika Bandaranaike Kumararunge, won the presidential elections. Since then, the new government has been eager to introduce liberal-democratic ideas into society through constitutional means as well as through efforts to involve civil society in governance.

Constitutional Responses

Sri Lanka's 1978 Constitution is in the process of being transformed into a liberal-democratic constitution that protects the
freedom of the individual. Security is not, however, the main
concern of the constitution-makers, who, like John Rawls,
claim that freedom is the highest good and that a rational
social order dedicated to principles of justice must strive to
realize them (Rawls, 1971). That men and women can aspire
to freedom only to the extent that their basic needs are met is
not sufficiently taken into consideration. Those basic needs
encompass the social goods that are essential to human
subsistence—food, clothing, housing, medical care, schooling.
Basic human needs imply the duty of government to satisfy
the welfare requirements, taking into account the constraints
of limited resources and the vagaries of natural disasters such
as drought and floods.[7]

The right to life, liberty, and security of person was expressly
stated in Chapter 6 of the 1972 Constitution, but there is no
comparable provision in the 1978 Constitution. In the current
constitution the various fundamental rights are not treated as
absolute but are subject to the limitations stated in Article 15.
National security, racial and religious harmony, parliamentary
privilege, contempt of court, defamation, public health, and
morality are among the recognized grounds for imposing
restrictions on fundamental rights (Goonesekere, 1988).

In the recently released draft constitution, the Chandrika
Kumaratunge government has rectified a number of deficiencies
of the present constitution. The right to life is an important
departure from the 1978 Constitution. Although security is con-
spicuously absent as a fundamental right, the draft constitution, which strengthens democratic institutions and provides an
enhanced protection of fundamental rights and freedoms,
implicitly acknowledges the importance of security (*Daily News*,
27 March 1997). Concurrent with the constitutional measures
have been attempts by the Chandrika Kumaratunge government to forge closer links with the dynamic non-governmental
organization (NGO) sector as a way of filling gaps left by
the state.[8]

Non-governmental Organizations and Security

There is evidence to suggest that the NGO sector has had an impact on government thinking about security. Indeed, the last 20 years have seen a rapid growth of indigenous NGOs in Sri Lanka.[9] The new emphasis on the NGO sector can be placed in the intellectual framework of wider changes in macro-economic policy, privatization, and the reduced role of the state in all aspects of the economy and provision of services. In the political realm, too, organizations that find inspiration in the values embedded in the Declaration of Human Rights and the International Covenant on Civil and Political Rights have emerged since the 1970s. Among the more active and influential Colombo-based NGOs are the following: the MARGA Institute, the International Center for Ethnic Studies, the Institute of Policy Studies, the Social Scientists' Association, the Movement for Inter-Racial Justice and Equality, the Center for Society and Religion, and the Center for Policy Alternatives. Until recently, governments have kept NGOs at a distance because they tend to critique the human rights record of the state. The change of government, however, saw an important change in the position of NGOs vis-à-vis the state. This change is partly due to the president's personal ties with intellectuals and human rights proponents, a bond that stems from her own intellectual interests. Unlike her predecessors, who were known for being anti-intellectual, Chandrika Kumaratunge has close links with the left-liberal intellectuals in Sri Lanka. Her political philosophy has evolved from socialism and a dependency-theory approach to world economics to a carefully modulated brand of liberalism with a human face. In drafting her political program prior to the elections of 1994, she relied on a think tank composed of university lecturers, journalists, and human rights activists who, like her, had started their journey in the left movement. This group of advisers constitutes an important human rights lobby within the government, and they have undoubtedly influenced the government's approach to security.

It is generally accepted that the political package for devolution of power—a plan that entails the division of the country into seven regions—was drafted as a political solution to the ethnic conflict by a team spearheaded by G.L. Peiris, former professor of law and former vice chancellor of the University of Colombo, with the special input by the late Dr Neelan Tiruchelvam, member of Parliament and director of the International Center for Ethnic Studies. Both men appear to be committed to the values of human rights and promote a human rights discourse that goes a considerable distance beyond the liberal-freedom discourse that was in vogue in the 1980s. Some of the president's close advisers speak a humanist language of human rights, which acknowledges the basic need for security as well as for freedom and which links the two basic value claims within theories of social and international justice. In Sri Lanka, the post-liberal struggle for human rights is linked more and more with the struggle for peace and economic-political development.

The NGOs' intervention in security matters invariably revolves around the notion of peace in the country as a precondition to the security of all its citizens. Middle-class elements such as the radical intelligentsia who work in the NGO sector and the progressive human rights community adhere to Western-style rationalist doctrines of equality but also uphold the individual's right to liberty and life. They see this as a necessary element of a peaceful society, a *sama samajaya*. Thousands of peace and human rights activists, representatives of more than 40 non-party formations and NGOs, staged a mass peace rally on 9 December 1994—the eve of International Human Rights Day. The procession was accompanied by street theater artistes who sang, danced, and portrayed the horrors of war and the joys of peace. The crowds were kept absorbed by speeches on various themes pertaining to peace, democracy, and human rights. The peace rally ended with the lighting of torches and the formal adoption of two appeals, one to the government and the other to the LTTE (*Tamil Times*, 15 January 1995). In the following years many such rallies championed by local NGOs have taken place.

Today most NGOs concerned with human rights still support the devolution of power to regions suggested by the government as a long-term solution to the ethnic conflict, while advising the government to refrain from military action that could harm the civilian population in Jaffna. Together with associations that share the same commitment to human rights and freedom such as the Peace Council and the Free Media Movement they act as watchguards to the government and often intervene when the government oversteps its powers. In that sense although Colombo based and with little mass appeal they form a powerful lobby owing to their links with Western governments and funding organizations and the international media.

On other fronts, dissatisfaction is brewing. Six years after the change of government there is a clear discrepancy between, on the one hand, people's expectations for a state that will protect them and, on the other, the liberal free-market approach adopted by the new regime in its dealings with labor problems.

Critiques of the State's Approach

Both the state's approach to security and the NGOs' approach are challenged on many fronts. The state is criticized specifically for its failure to include cultural and economic elements in its conception of security. Those outside the government are concerned with threats of a non-military character—external domination of the country's economy, dependence on other countries for scientific research and technology, and the unrestricted penetration of Western values through the media resulting in an erosion and eventual loss of national identity. For a sizable group of people, security cannot refer simply to the preservation of the state's independence and territorial integrity. The NGO approach to security is criticized insofar as it is grounded in human rights and universalism, notions generally associated with the West.

Insurgent groups such as the JVP list a range of problems, including the threat posed by capitalism to the culture and traditions of the Sinhalese people and the government's submissive attitude to the dictates of lending institutions. Other pressure groups such as trade unions argue that the state has sold out to international capitalism and failed to protect its children from want. Religious groupings such as the powerful Buddhist Sangha criticize the state's approach for subordinating culture and religion to economic and political concerns and in the same vein the NGO sector for pandering to the demands of Western funding agencies. Do these voices influence in any way the state's conception of security?

The Context: Liberalization and Privatization

In 1977, Sri Lanka opened up its economy after more than a decade of import control. Chandrika Kumaratunge came to power with a promise to the financial world that her government would not reverse the liberalization and privatization program of the previous government. The People's Alliance's political program, however, was more ambivalent about the privatization issue. Although it clearly accepted the inevitability of a market economy, it stated that 'public utilities which are essential for day-to-day life must function under government control, but with adequate autonomy for efficient management' (Gooneratne and Karunaratne, 1994: 12). Thus although the People's Alliance maintained its commitment to the privatization program begun in the previous regime, its manifesto emphasized a people-oriented approach to social and political reforms. People, the manifesto argued, matter more than reasons of state. In its election manifesto the government had stated that health, education, water, electricity, highways and railway, airports, irrigation, main state banks, and public-sector insurance establishments must function under government control (ibid.: 12). But in February 1996 it was revealed that the government was considering the privatization of no fewer than 70 state institutions. Among the enterprises earmarked for divestment of shares were the State Mortgage and Investment Bank, the Independent Television Network, the Ceylon Shipping Corporation, and Air Lanka (*Sunday Times*, 2 June 1996). The government's inability or refusal to keep its electoral promises has led to challenges from labor and to a growing feeling that the government has duped its supporters.

Security as Social Justice

Paradoxically, the JVP insurrection of 1987–89 started in the name of national security defined in a manner very similar to the state's conception. Its manifesto proposed that 'a new foreign policy will be adopted to ensure the national independence and territorial integrity of Sri Lanka'. The JVP's approach was, in fact, a combination of two perceptions of security. On the one hand, it claimed to be the savior of a nation that was then enduring external threats and internal conflict. This vision of national security was in no way different from that of the diplomats and mainstream academics. On the other hand, the JVP articulated a conception of security whereby the state would protect and look after the people.

In 1988, the JVP Action Center issued a communique calling the masses to protest against the J.R. Jayawardena–Rajiv Gandhi accord, which brought about provincial councils and devolution of power. The rhetoric was one of justice and equality rather than rights: 'We shall not keep quiet when the patriots in the South who fight for equality and justice are massacred by mercenaries. We shall not wait patiently when the reasonable struggle by the students—our future generation—for justice and equality is repressed brutally' (Gunaratne, 1990: 291). The idea that basic needs are contained in the concept of security is reflected in the notion of rights embodied in the JVP vision of a *sadharanaya lokaya* ('equitable world') where the poor are not discriminated against and social justice prevails. In 1987–89, a primary component of its vision of social justice was the notion of mass universal education as a basic human right. In the economic field, foreign trade, internal wholesale trade, and heavy industry would be maintained as state monopolies. Foreign banks and financial institutions would be nationalized. A radical land reform would be implemented. The ethnic problem would be dealt with by ensuring that equality prevailed among all races in education and land distribution.

The JVP took it upon itself to secure social justice among the Sinhalese by taking up arms against what it saw as an oppressive state. It argued that the Sri Lankan state since independence had been committed to welfarism—that is, to safeguard the basic needs of its citizens. After 1977, however, the economy was opened and industrial growth based on foreign investment was encouraged. A necessary concomitant to such an export-led strategy was the World Bank and International Monetary Fund's (IMF) 'structural adjustment policies', which demanded a shifting of public resources away from social welfare into investment. The JVP opposed the system of private property on the grounds that a society based on humanistic principles can never be built on a capitalist framework. The socialization of property relations was firmly defended. The JVP claimed that Sri Lanka had a neocolonial economy completely subservient to the imperialists. In this view capitalism, which has led to neo-colonial domination and an erosion of traditional mores and values, is the main enemy (ibid.: 259–66). One of the primary global threats, according to the radical nationalists, is the involvement of lending institutions such as the World Bank and the IMF in running the country, especially in light of their demands for 'good governance'.

Significance of the JVP Alternative

Until recently, governments have ignored these voices from below. But after two insurrections and thousands of dead, the problems of the poor unemployed youth of the south can no longer be ignored. Although the JVP movement was violently crushed in the late 1980s, its ideas remain popular in certain circles such as the student movement and some trade unions. Militant Sinhala groups such as the proponents of a *jathika chintanaya* (national ideology), student movements such as the Janata Mithuro (Friends of the People), and trade unions have offered their own definition of security—a definition that involves a critique of the state in Sri Lanka as a component of global capitalism. Many young men and women interviewed for this study expressed, if not allegiance to the JVP, at least an intellectual affinity with its ideas. A well-known social critic, Gunadasa Ameresekere, has put forward the concept of *jathika arthikaya*, a national or indigenous economy. His vision idealizes the village and rural culture and castigates the open economy without clearly advocating an alternative model of development. The Janata Mithuro envisages an environment-friendly regime that would control the pernicious effects of modernization—tourism, pollution, urbanization. These approaches reflect the need for security from 'imperialist/global threats' and for turning inward to focus on indigenous culture rather than international conceptions of human rights. More recently the National Movement Against Terrorism (NMAT) denigrates all moves made by the peace lobby to reach for a negotiated peace settlement between the state and the LTTE and calls for a military solution to the Tamil problem. They vilify 'foreign funded NGOs' as responsible for undermining the morale of the troops and pursuing selfish aims instead of thinking of the good of the nation. With each military setback these voices gain more momentum and a new circle of power is emerging that harbors diametrically opposite views to those of the NGOs. In that sense these two circles feed on each other while competing for the attention of the state.

Until now, however, the state's approach to security has little in common with the JVP/anti-systemic critique, which challenges the foundation of society itself and the belief that Western-style economic and political liberalism represents 'the good society' (Lipset, 1960: 403). No government will agree to reverse the ongoing process of liberalization in order to appease the JVP or its supporters. But under pressure from these anti-capitalist forces, the state can be forced to change its policy on certain issues. Thus one could say that the JVP/anti-systemic ideology, when used in a limited manner, may have some impact—as in the recent Ceylon Electricity Board strike. In that case the state had to compromise in order to assure workers that privatization would not take place at the expense of their interests. Here one can say that the voice of anti-systemic groups did have an impact on the state's approach to security. Through strikes, pickets, and representations, these groups act as watchdogs that now and then remind the government of its commitment to human security.

The Sangha's Critique

According to Sinhala-Buddhist tradition, fashioned largely by the ancient chronicles of the island, Sri Lanka is the *dharma-dvipa* (island of the faith) consecrated by the Buddha himself as the land in which his teachings would flourish. One such chronicle, *Mahavamsa*, states that on the very day of the Buddha's death, Vijaya, the founder of the Sinhala race, landed in Sri Lanka as if to bear witness to the Buddha's prediction (Geiger, 1950). The king was traditionally the protector of Buddhism, and after independence the new nation-state took over this function. Every constitution of the country since 1972 has stressed the special place given to Buddhism, the religion of more than 70 per cent of the population. Buddhism is in Sri Lanka a legitimizing, integrative, and moral force that governments and politicians must take into account. Although Buddhism is protected by the state and practiced by the vast majority of people, many of its proponents present it as a religion under threat. The threat has been portrayed as coming from various places at different times. In the 1950s, Buddhist leaders complained of the influence of 'Catholic action' and spearheaded the Sri Lanka Freedom Party (SLFP) campaign, taking over denominational schools, evicting Catholic nursing nuns, giving Buddhist preachers more time over national radio, and securing employment for Buddhists in the higher echelons of the administration and armed services. This was, in fact, a process of rectifying perceived colonial favoritism to Catholics.

Since independence, political monks organized in pressure groups have taken positions on crucial issues, and they influence people by virtue of their moral prestige. When the UNP came to power and liberalized the economy, monks protested against the growing consumerism. The same groups protested against the signing of the Indo-Sri Lankan Accord in 1987, claiming that the agreement betrayed the Sinhala people by conceding too much to the Tamils and allowing Indians to enter the island as a peacekeeping force. The rhetoric of betrayal, and of the need to protect the land, are ever-present elements in the Sinhala nationalist discourse where Sinhalese and Buddhist identities are merged into one. The threat is identified as coming from the West, Christianity, and capitalism.

The phenomenon of religious influence was particularly apparent a few years ago when a book published by Stanley Tambiah, *Buddhism Betrayed? Religion, Politics and Violence in Sri Lanka* (1992), became the center of a controversy. It was alleged in the Sinhala press that with the publication of the book an international conspiracy had been launched: the co-conspirators included the World Institute for Development Economic Research (WIDER), its former director, and the United Nations organizations; the chief beneficiary of the plot was the LTTE. This controversy, and the response of the reading public in Sri Lanka, showed that quite a few people believe that American imperialism is behind most of the evils of the world and that a number of traitors in Sri Lanka—especially intellectuals with local and foreign NGO links—have sold out to the West. A few months later the government, bowing to the pressure of the Sangha, imposed a ban on the import and sale of the book. This was a major setback for the non-governmental sector that had issued a statement calling for the respect of the freedom of expression notwithstanding the content of the book.

The Buddhist Sangha plays an important role in fostering such ideas, because many Buddhists look to the leaders among the sects of Buddhist monks in Sri Lanka as moral guides even on temporal matters. The condemnation by many influential monks of the devolution package—a proposal offered to the Tamil people by Chandrika Bandaranaike Kumaratunge's government—as a threat to the unitary character of the state seems to have dampened the initial enthusiasm of its promoters. On 5 March 1996, a vast gathering of the Buddhist order, numbering more than 2,000 members, assembled to denounce the government's proposals to defuse the ethnic problem. A prominent scholar-monk, the venerable Dr Walpola Rahula, made the following statement: 'These devolution proposals could only cause chaos and doom to the country and hence the package should be rejected in toto' (*The Island*, 6 March 1996). When the Sangha believes the state is failing to protect the majority culture, language, and religion of the land or is endangering the sovereignty of the country, it voices its opinion in the media. The state is then obliged to take the Sangha's view into account even if it does not always reflect the view of the majority.

Conclusion

Today as the battle for Jaffna is claiming more and more lives security appears to be a contested notion around which new circles of power have emerged. The non-governmental sector which often speaks in the name of an elusive civil society is pressing for the respect for human rights by the state and the LTTE and stressing the need for peace. Sinhalese patriots grouped in anti-terrorism movements or new political parties such as the Sihala Urumaya (Sinhalese heritage) have begun to openly accuse the state of weakness and of playing into the hands of the LTTE and the foreign hegemonic forces that support it. Their notion of security is subsumed in a global critique of capitalism and a naive anti-foreign rhetoric. Underlying their political vision is an attempt to find new democratic forms not thought out by the post-Enlightenment social consensus of the secularized Christian world. The Western-oriented non-governmental sector is quite logically included in the forces to be fought against by these new forces in political society.

Facing criticism from the NGO sector as well as from new political movements the state remains committed to a concept of security that means protecting the sovereignty of the territory in the north and east and protecting the people in the south from terrorist acts by using the services of the security forces. For the people of the Jaffna peninsula, however, security means security both from the state and from the LTTE. For the Tamils in Colombo, some of whom are arbitrarily arrested in anticipation of terrorist activities, there is no security from the counterinsurgent state.

More than ever, security is a complex concept with a multiplicity of faces.

Notes

1. Most works on security in Sri Lanka focus exclusively on the foreign policy and strategic role of Sri Lanka in South Asia. See, for instance, Shelton U. Kodikara (1990) and S.D. Muni (1993).
2. This survey on perceptions of security is based on a sample of 100 people and was carried out in December 1995. It was not done according to strict sociological methods of surveying, because its purpose was mainly to get a qualitative assessment of perceptions of security.
3. See, for instance, A.J. Wilson (1979), Rohan Gunaratna (1990), and C.A. Chandraprema (1991).
4. See, for instance, the Report of the Working Group on Enforced or Involuntary Disappearances (7–18 October, 1991), Commission on Human Rights, 48th session, 8 January, 1992.
5. From a survey on conceptions of security: Interviews of a sample of 35 Sinhalese males and 35 Sinhalese females.
6. From a survey on perceptions of security: Interviews of 10 Tamil males and 9 Tamil females, December 1995.

7. Christian Bay (1987: 129) has argued in an absorbing article that security is the poor person's freedom. He goes on to say: 'For people who are heavily oppressed, whether by political design or economic circumstances, or both, their measure of individual security determines the size of their limited space for freedom of choice.'

8. After the 1999 elections to the northwestern provincial council, NGOs engaged in election monitoring severely condemned the violence associated with the campaign as well as the malpractices essentially committed by state-sponsored elements before and during election day. This has led to a breakdown in the relationship between the government and the human rights NGOs.

9. This section draws on Sunil Bastian (1988: 12–18).

References

Bastian, Sunil. 1988. 'NGOs in Development', *Thatched Patio*, Vol. 18 (April): 12–18.

Bay, Christian. 1987. 'Conceptions of Security: Individual, National and Global', in Bhikku Parekh and Thomas Pantham (eds), *Political Discourse: Explorations in Indian and Western Political Thought*. New Delhi: Sage.

Chandraprema, C.A. 1991. *Sri Lanka, the Years of Terror: The JVP Insurrection 1987–1989*. Colombo: Lake House.

Chari, P.R. 1987. 'Security Aspects of Indian Foreign Policy', in Stephen P. Cohen (ed.), *The Security of South Asia: American and Asian Perspectives*, pp. 50–60. Urbana: University of Illinois Press.

Dumont, Louis. 1970. *Religion, Politics and History in India*. The Hague: Mouton.

Geiger, Wilhelm. 1950. *The Mahavamsa*. Colombo: Government Information Department (translated)

Giddens, Anthony. 1985. *A Contemporary Critique of Historical Materialism, Vol. 2, The Nation State and Violence*. Cambridge, Mass: Polity Press.

Gooneratne, W.G. and **K.S. Karunaratne.** 1994. 'Election Manifesto of the People's Alliance—Parliamentary General Elections', Tenth Parliament of Sri Lanka, pp. 85–120. Colombo: Associated Newspapers of Ceylon Ltd.

Goonesekere, R.K.W. 1988. *Fundamental Rights and the Constitution: A Case Book*. Colombo: Law and Society Trust/Open University.

Gunaratne, Rohan. 1990. *Sri Lanka: A Lost Revolution: The Inside Story of the JVP*. Kandy: Institute of Fundamental Studies.

Kanapatipillai, Valli. 1990. 'July 1983: The Survivors' Experience' in Veena Das (ed.), *Mirrors of Violence*. New Delhi: Oxford University Press.

Keerawella, Gamini B. 1990. 'Peace and Security Perceptions of a Small State: Sri Lanka Responses to Superpower Naval Rivalry in the Indian Ocean 1970–77', in Shelton U. Kodikara (ed.), *South Asian Strategic Issues: Sri Lanka Perspectives*. New Delhi: Sage.

Kodikara, Shelton U. (ed.). 1990. *South Asian Strategic Issues: Sri Lanka Perspectives*. New Delhi: Sage.

———. 1993. *External Compulsions of South Asian Politics*. New Delhi: Sage.

Lipset, S.M. 1960. *Political Man*. London: Mercury.

Muni, S.D. 1993. *Pangs of Proximity: India and Sri Lanka's Ethnic Conflict*. New Delhi: National Publishing House.

Nandy, Ashis. 1994. 'Culture, Voice and Development: A Primer for the Unsuspecting', *Thesis Eleven*, Vol. 39.

Nissan, Elisabeth. 1996. *Sri Lanka: A Bitter Harvest*. London: Minority Rights Group International.

Rabinow, Paul (ed.). 1984. *The Foucault Reader*. New York: Pantheon.

Rawls, John. 1971. *A Theory of Justice*. Cambridge Mass.: Harvard University Press.

Rosenau, James N. 1994. 'New Dimensions of Security: The Interaction of Globalizing and Localizing Forces', *Security Dialogue*, No. 25(3): 255–81.

Sen, Amartya. 1990. *On Ethics and Economics*. New Delhi: Oxford University Press.

Uyangoda, Jayadeva. 1989. 'The Indo-Lanka Accord of July 1987 and the State in Sri Lanka', in Shelton U. Kodikara (ed.), *Indo-Sri Lanka Agreement of July 1987*. Colombo: International Relations Program, University of Colombo.

Warnapala, W.A. Wiswa. 1994. *Ethnic Strife and Politics in Sri Lanka: An Investigation into Demands and Responses*. New Delhi: Navrang.

Werake, Mahinda and **P.V.J. Jayasekera.** 1995. *Security Dilemma of a Small State, Part II, Internal Crisis and External Intervention in Sri Lanka*. Kandy: Institute for International Studies.

Wickramasinghe, Nira. 1995. *Ethnic Politics in Colonial Sri Lanka*. New Delhi: Vikas.

Wilson, A.J. 1979. *Politics in Sri Lanka, 1947–1979*. London: Macmillan, 2 ed.

Chapter 2

Good Governance and the New Aid Regime

Introduction

When nineteenth-century ideas of 'imperial power' gave way after the collapse of colonial rule to the notion of international responsibility and the birth of the United Nations, the 'white man's burden' needed a new justification[1]—and the aid regime was born. South Asia today is part of the interdependent world that emerged after World War II from the Bretton Woods agreements of 1944 providing for the establishment of the World Bank and the International Monetary Fund. For example, the industrialization of Pakistan since independence has largely depended on foreign aid and private foreign investment. The economy of Bangladesh also rests on handouts of foreign aid, which have failed significantly to improve that nation's abysmal standard of living. Sri Lanka relies on export revenues from the sale of primary products—garments have replaced tea as the prime export—displaying a similar network of external economic ties and dependence (Ghosh, 1990: 338–39). The movement of capital, ideas, technologies, and persons has reduced the real importance of statehood and dramatically eroded the significance of nominal state sovereignty.

The volume of aid to the less developed countries (LDCs) has grown at a phenomenal rate. In the early 1950s, aid from all sources was less than $11.8 million. Supported by a United Nations (UN) campaign urging member states to give at least 0.7 per cent of gross national product (GNP) as aid, today's total disbursements amount to $60 billion.[2] As the volume of aid increased, taxpayers in developed countries began to demand that their contributions should not support regimes that failed to respect the human rights of their citizens. They also learned that in many instances aid was not trickling down to the people.[3]

This has led in recent decades to an increasing concern for human rights issues in the principal donor countries. By 'human rights' is meant those civil, political, economic, social, and cultural rights embodied in the Universal Declaration of Human Rights and the International Covenants that were promulgated by the United Nations and to which most countries of the world have subscribed. In signing these covenants states accept that human rights are an international responsibility and that governments are accountable not only to their own citizens but to the world community as well. They willingly concede a share of their state sovereignty. Many now recognize that consideration of human rights should and does affect the provision of aid and development assistance (Tomasevski, 1989). As will be shown, the human rights discourse is itself subject to national security interests, and is in the process of being displaced and supplanted by another and more perverse ideological discourse, that of 'good governance', which is fast becoming a new orthodoxy in official Western aid policy and on Third World thinking development (Leftwich, 1993: 605).

The issue of human rights and foreign policy will be examined briefly before considering the linkages that existed between aid and human rights in the context of bilateral and multilateral aid relationships until the end of the 1980s. Consideration will then be given to the shift that has occurred from a total lack of concern for human rights on the part of multilateral aid agencies and from a serious concern for individual human rights on the part of donor countries to a more complex and interventionist approach embodied in the notion of 'good governance' and 'political conditionality'. In this new approach, the aim is nothing less than to change the world system by reforming the fundamental institutions of the recipient state.

Human Rights and Aid: Negative Linkages in the 1990s

Human Rights and Foreign Policy

Kautiliya, the ancient Indian political theorist, conceptualized six different categories of policies for handling interstate relations: peace, war, indifference, strengthening one's position, subordinating an ally or vassal, and duplicity. Concern whether development assistance should be linked to a country's observance of human rights stems from perplexity among the public in aid-dispensing countries over the duplicity of their government's aid policies, which at certain times seem indifferent to the plight of starving masses and at other times spell a readiness to intervene for hardly commendable reasons. This debate reflects apprehension that repressive regimes may maintain their power through foreign aid, using it as an instrument of legitimation to strengthen and perpetuate their position. Clearly, ideological or geopolitical considerations on the part of donor countries have often overridden moral concerns, as in the case of the support given by the United States to Pakistan during the period of martial law in that country or in US dealings with Central American dictatorships.

The experience of the US as a large donor country serves to illustrate the linkage between aid and foreign policy. As Stansfield Turner has pointedly observed, 'The most obvious specific impact of the new world order is that except for Soviet nuclear weaponry, the preeminent threat to U.S. national security now lies in the economic sphere' (Turner, 1991: 151). The end of the Cold War loosed US foreign policy from its moorings, requiring a thorough reorientation of aid strategy. Indeed, as James C. Clad recently wrote, 'After 45 years America's foreign bilateral assistance program lies dead in the water' (Clad and Stone, 1992–93: 196). Without communism to contain, the US has had to reassess and readjust its aid programs.

Since the end of World War II, there has been a series of ideologically inspired shifts in aid policy. Throughout the Cold War, US priorities in foreign aid were conditioned by national security concerns, creating an important linkage between foreign policy and foreign aid. The first subsumed the second. Before the collapse of the USSR, aid was given to friendly non-communist countries, particularly those forming a political buffer against the Soviet empire. Even strategically insignificant countries were affected. Sri Lanka was at this time governed by the left-wing government of Sirimavo Bandaranaike, which nationalized Western oil and other business facilities. The US reacted immediately by cutting its aid program to Sri Lanka, including the provision of milk and buns to school-children. An important shift occurred under President Jimmy Carter who, building on efforts of the US Congress, established the legitimacy of human rights as a distinct concern, although the success of this upgrading was not apparent until after Carter had left office. Human rights became a factor in his administration's decisions about providing economic aid, and legislation was adopted to reflect this. But the belief that human rights must yield to national security interests imposed limitations on the policy. Carter's approach was (in the words of a State Department official) 'imperfect but honest'.[4]

The second shift in US aid orientation occurred when President Ronald Reagan appropriated human rights (viewed as the embodiment of Western values) for his ideological crusade against communism. Reagan's successor, President George Bush, also linked aid and human rights selectively, but with less impunity than Reagan (Orenlichter, 1992: 340–52). A comparison of the per capita Overseas Development Assistance (ODA) received by democratic and authoritarian regimes points to the gulf between rhetoric and reality. The relationship between aid and human rights in the 1980s has been quite rightly described as 'perverse' (UNDP, 1994: 76). US President Bill Clinton's China policy also illustrates how foreign policy considerations and economic motives often override human rights concerns.

It can be argued that during the Cold War the linkage between aid and human rights was only a single element in a multipronged foreign policy in which covert international war was practiced on many occasions against elected governments deemed unsupportive of US interests, and, therefore, outside the circle of democratic communities. Iran in 1953, Guatemala in 1954, Indonesia in 1957, Brazil from 1961, Chile in 1973, and Nicaragua from 1984 are the most striking examples (Forsythe, 1993: 33–54). In these cases, the US organized or aided covert interventions involving violence because it was felt that American national security was at stake. In countries where intervention was not possible or not crucial, aid linked to human rights was deemed sufficient as a foreign policy instrument.

Most Western European donor countries (with the exception of Nordic states) have followed the pattern of the United States, turning a blind eye to human rights abuses when committed by friendly countries, as in France's acquiescence in Emperor Bokassa's murderous reign in Central Africa. French protégé Mobutu Sese Seko in Zaire owned 51 Mercedes-Benz cars when he dismissed 7,000 school teachers from the Zairian school system on the grounds that there was no money to pay their salaries. Despite such outrages, his government remained for many years one of the most favored recipients of Western aid in Africa. The degree and nature of the distortion vary from donor state to donor state. The influx of refugees from the south into Europe has added a twist to the human rights issue. European countries seeking to rid themselves of refugees, such as Switzerland, must refrain from even mentioning the human rights situation in the country of return. This contributes to the cynical application of human rights standards for reasons of political expediency.

Negative Linkages Aid

Among the instruments available within the framework of development cooperation for the purpose of influencing, promoting, and maintaining human rights, it is possible to differentiate between 'positive measures' geared to improving the human rights situation and 'negative measures' as a response to gross and systematic violations of human rights.

Negative measures consist of using aid as a political weapon. There are many gradations: funding can be conditioned on certain improvements in observance of human rights, a cut-off may be threatened, and finally aid may be withheld. Sanctions have worked in South Africa but not in war-ridden Bosnia. The effectiveness of the policy depends on the credibility of the threat; the relative size of the donor's aid package; and, most important, on the nature of the recipient regime and its susceptibility to this form of manipulation. There is also the danger that the withdrawal of development assistance might lead to worse hardships for the population. One illustration of this is what happened in Ethiopia. Following the establishment of a Marxist regime and a brutal period of revolutionary purges, Western donors cut off long-term development assistance in 1977, limiting the aid package to emergency relief. The discontinuation of aid was one of the factors contributing to the famine of 1984 (Kettaneh, 1990).

In the case of Sri Lanka, such linkage has become commonplace. Since 1983 the country has been the theater of a bitter ethnic war that is compromising the economic recovery that began in 1977 after a long period of stagnation and brought a decade of development based on protectionism and import substitution. The Sri Lankan state and Tamil militant groups are engaged in violent acts that discourage foreign investment and try the patience of human rights organizations. But, the government's renewed commitment to giving priority to private initiative in a market economy has produced a real growth of 6 per cent in the 1990s. This growth has been fueled by a massive public investment program, largely financed by foreign assistance. Multilateral aid to Sri Lanka is of two types: outright grants and loans on concessionary terms. Both grant aid and concessionary loans come from Western Europe, the US, Japan, and international organizations. Most foreign aid is pledged at the meetings of the Aid Sri Lanka Consortium, which is organized by the World Bank on behalf of the major donor countries. The Sri Lanka government sends the World Bank an annual request outlining its needs. The member donors then meet to consider these requests and coordinate their aid policies.

Sri Lanka's recent past has been marked by frequent occurrences of torture and deaths in custody, extrajudicial killings, and reprisal massacres. Arbitrary arrests and detentions for long periods are also common. Sri Lanka has been under a state of emergency since 1983 except for a period of five months. In 1994, the new left-of-center government of Chandrika Kumaratunge lifted the emergency in the south. In the north and the east, the security forces are still invested with extraordinary powers under the Emergency Regulations and the Prevention of Terrorism Act (PTA).[5] Partly as a response to the human rights situation and partly because of non-utilization of funds—a substantial portion of the aid provisions (funds earmarked for the rehabilitation of the north and northeast provinces for 1989–90) was not spent because of the military situation— many donors decided not to increase their budgets for 1990–91. Donor pressure since April 1990, after the death of Richard de Soyza, a prominent journalist, has resulted in an improvement in the human rights situation. The fact is that by placing conditions on aid, aid-giving governments putting pressure on Sri Lanka to improve its human rights record is not seen as a loss-of-sovereignty problem by many human rights activists.[6] Indeed they argue that when nations subscribe to the International Covenant on Civil and Political Rights, and the International Covenant on Economic, Social, and Cultural Rights they agree in effect to cede a part of their sovereignty. Governments have agreed to answer to the UN Commission on Human Rights and to the Human Rights Committee. The first institution is composed of about 50 members appointed by governments selected by the United Nations Economic and Social Council. The second, set up under the Covenant on Civil and Political Rights, is a group of persons elected by the parties to the covenant and serving as individuals.

In the north European countries where interest in human rights has been strongest and its translation into political acts most immediate, the main concern has been to avoid accusations of sovereign interference. The states' formal position has been that aid should relate to the needs of people and not to the conduct of their governments. But in reality Norway has been taking human rights considerations into account since 1986 and Denmark since 1987. Donor countries, and especially the Nordic states, rely on the reports and statements of both international organs and non-state-level organizations before forming their policy on aid. All governments have to submit regular five-year reports to the United Nations. Sri Lanka's turn was in 1991, and the representative of the government had a difficult time at the hearings. The Commission on Human Rights may receive representations and (when it deems necessary) send working groups and rapporteurs to investigate the situation in a country. In 1991, a Working Group on Disappearances visited Sri Lanka. The Sri Lanka government agreed to accept and implement most of the group's recommendations and encouraged further visits in order that an external evaluation could be effected. Among other measures, the government appointed a Presidential Commission on Disappearances to investigate complaints and set up a Human Rights Task Force.[7] Other organizations concerned with the advancement and promotion of human rights such as Asia Watch and the International Commission of Jurists exert similar pressure on the government. The concern that donor countries will cut or reduce aid puts the government in a situation where it is answerable to them as well. In the period before the aid meeting, the government acts with a certain amount of circumspection.

In 1985, Margaret Thatcher became the first European leader to attempt, if unsuccessfully, to build human rights conditions into the provisions for European Community (EC) aid to Africa, the Caribbean, and Pacific countries under the Lomé Conventions. Although that attempt was initially rejected by ACP leaders as an unwarranted infringement on their domestic sovereignty, by the time of the Lomé IV Convention of 1990 an explicit reference to human rights in the context of EC aid could no longer be avoided (Clapham, 1993: 432). More recently, the European Union has, because of its high level on internal cohesion, been fairly successful at linking human rights and development. A recent example is the freezing of Lomé IV funds to Sudan by the European Commission based on a recommendation resulting from a European Parliamentary resolution. The reason given was the existence of widespread human rights abuses.

UN Human Rights and Development: Parallel Processes

There is a clear division of tasks and responsibilities between the agencies in the UN system that deal specifically with human rights (the Human Rights Commission, the General Assembly, and the Secretariat) and those that come under the broad heading of the promotion of social and economic rights. Although multilateral institutions of the UN such as the World Health Organization (WHO) and the United Nations Development Program (UNDP) have adopted development policies based on human needs, they are not articulated using rights language (Kettaneh, 1990). The first Human Development Report did show some innovation by trading the newly minted concept of 'economic development' for the concept of 'human development'.

In the field, it is clear that human rights considerations are not taken into account in the context of UN development assistance. Aid is channeled in an indiscriminate way to countries governed by regimes that violate human rights. The question today is whether the UN has a mandate to make its aid conditional on the human rights situation in the recipient country. Article 2 (7) of the Charter of the UN is quite explicit:

Nothing contained in the present Charter shall authorize the United Nations to intervene in matters which are essentially within the domestic jurisdiction of any state or shall require the Members to submit such matters to settlement under the present Charter; but this principle shall not prejudice the application of enforcement measures under Chapter VII (United Nations, 1993: 5).

Although Article 2 (1) of the charter reflects very clearly the duty of states and the organization to refrain from intervention in each other's internal affairs—'the Organization is based on the principle of the sovereign equality of all its members'—the collective voice of sovereign states in the context of deliberations of the legislative body of the General Assembly has often stigmatized certain individual states. Indeed the prohibition in Article 2 (7) is qualified by its reference to 'enforcement measures under Chapter VII' (i.e., the chapter dealing with the powers of the Security Council to maintain or restore international peace and security) (Damrosh, 1993: 275–94). Arguably, the application of sanctions in the form of an arms embargo against apartheid regimes (for which the council took an inclusive view of 'threats to peace' in order to act under Chapter VII) is another form of collective enforcement of human rights obligations. Article 41 of the charter grants the Security Council the power to impose trade embargoes for the maintenance of international peace and security. Trade sanctions have until now been applied sparingly and only in very extreme cases of human rights abuses, such as Iraq's treatment of its Kurdish population. What is necessary is to build on precedents and go beyond them by formulating a mechanism by which the UN development agencies together with the UN human rights agencies follow an integrated and principled approach that links development aid to human rights and is applied to all countries receiving UN assistance.[8]

Good Governance and Aid Conditionality

Positive Linkages

When aid is used as an instrument to improve observance of human rights in recipient country, one speaks of positive linkages. This entails intervening directly to rectify situations that are judged detrimental to a human rights regime. The current concept of good governance would not have been possible without the prior acceptance of positive linkages by the world community.

It is crucial, at the outset, to distinguish between governments and the non-governmental organizations (NGOs) as recipients of aid. The reason why many countries engage in the promotion of human rights within the government sector is that they consider this a middle road between the two extreme situations of withholding aid and direct support for an often ideologically hostile human rights sector. The US, for instance, tends to channel assistance directly through the government. But increasingly, the trend is for more aid to be channeled through NGOs.

The number of indigenous NGOs involved in human rights work has increased over the last decade as the tendency for donors to channel their development funding in this way becomes more pronounced (Asian Cultural Forum, 1993). The last 20 years has seen a rapid growth of indigenous NGOs in Sri Lanka.[9] Most NGOs combine elements of service delivery with elements of community mobilization. Most bilateral and multilateral aid programs make explicit allocations of resources for NGOs. This is partly a response to the equity concerns of the donors' domestic constituents regarding recipient government utilization of foreign funds. The new emphasis on the non-governmental sector reflects the intellectual framework of wider changes in macroeconomic policy, privatization and the reduced role of states in all aspects of the economy and in the provision of services. NGOs are seen as a dynamic privatized alternative to bloated state bureaucracies.

The change in aid policy by the Danish government reflects this new emphasis. Denmark cut off aid to Sri Lanka at the end of 1989 when the Colombo government, in its attempt to put down the insurrection of the People's Liberation Front (JVP), encouraged massive human rights abuses. When aid was resumed in 1993, Denmark proposed to upgrade Sri Lanka to 'Country Program' status while assisting it in improving human rights and democratic freedoms. This meant that aid to developmental projects would be resumed once the first aim was achieved. Individuals and groups closer to the grassroots would be supported in efforts to promote ethnic harmony or to promote press freedom. The Sri Lanka government was indignant at these proposals, which were likened to a 'Trojan horse' being introduced by strategies in Sri Lanka to monitor and meddle in its internal human rights affairs (*Counterpoint*, April–May 1994: 26–28).

The rise of the non-govermental sector, which is often equated with prodemocracy movements, together with the collapse of official communist regimes and the resurgence of neoliberalism, explain the new concern with 'governance' and democracy (Leftwich, 1993: 606) on the part of the World Bank and some donor countries.

Good Governance and the World Bank: The Primacy of Economic Issues

The World Bank has, on the whole, shown very little concern for human rights issues. Until recently, the same structural impediments to human rights/development linkage that existed in the UN system also existed within the World Bank system. The major difference lies in the decision-making authority, of the bank, where voting power is weighted according to the size of the donor's contribution. At present, the World Bank has 148 member countries. As with the International Monetary Fund (IMF), some members have more say than others. The 'big five' control 42 per cent of the votes and the industrial countries together 60 per cent of the votes of the board of executive directors (Green et al., 1990: 14). This concentrates power in the Western states and allows for political/ideological motivations to influence fund allocation. For example, Vietnam was not eligible for World Bank funds because of a US veto. The freeze on bank funds to China following the killings of June 1989 is also evidence of an awareness of the development/human rights linkage.

The majority of World Bank funds (roughly 70 per cent) are disbursed as loans, the balance takes the form of concessionary loans through the International Development Assistance (IDA), as well as some technical assistance grants. In policy terms, this also means that funds are conditioned on the recipient's adoption of certain economic policies.

Recent works critical of the World Bank highlight three major shifts in its development policy. The 1950s and 1960s were characterized by large-scale infrastructure developments that required massive investments in capital projects. The bank primarily promoted planning and public sector initiatives providing for dams, schools, roads, and other infrastructure projects in the developing world. The underlying theory was that the LDC economies required a jump start after which they could 'take off' following the growth pattern of European states during the industrial revolution. The benefits of this accelerated growth could then trickle down to the poor. The realization that these predictions were not materializing led to a change in policy and a concentration on 'basic needs' in the 1970s. This included poverty alleviation, education, health, and nutrition. Sprawling, inefficient bureaucracies and a changing global economic climate led to a balance-of-payments crisis in the early 1980s and another change in development policy. The World Bank became a great proponent of competition, privatization, and markets (Gibbon, 1993: 28–35).

The World Bank and its main contributor, the US, began to use the concept of 'good governance' in the period from 1985 to 1989, when referring to forms of political management that included some aspects of political representation. It started as a critique of the African states suggesting deconstructive institutional reforms. Adrian Leftwich has pointed out that the first contemporary public appearance of the notion of good governance came in a World Bank report on Africa in 1989, which argued that, 'Underlying the litany of Africa's development problems is a crisis of governance' (Leftwich, 1993: 610–11; for more details see World Bank, 1989). It further defines governance as or the 'exercise of political power to manage a nation's affairs'. Good governance included some or all of the following features: an efficient public service; an independent judicial system and legal framework to enforce contracts; the accountable administration of public funds; an independent public auditor, responsible to a representative legislature; respect for the law and human rights at all levels of government; a pluralistic institutional structure and a free press (Leftwich, 1993: 610–11, 192). The World Bank, however, never endorsed the notion of political conditionality, as this would constitute a derogation of its purely technicist grounding. In 1992, a booklet was published in which governance was quite clearly redefined in terms of development policy, as separate from politics. The problem of governance is said to involve four distinct issues: poor public service management, lack of accountability, absence of a legal framework for development, and problems of information availability or transparency. The underlying assumption was that it is possible to have a technical 'solution' to these problems of governance that is independent of the form of political representation (Word Bank, 1992: 1).

The World Bank's lack of concern for the sanctity of representation has been highlighted in an analysis that correlates World Bank loans and democracy for the Philippines and Bangladesh. After these two countries lifted martial law, their shares in the total loans given by the World Bank declined (UNDP, 1994: 76). Clearly, martial law regimes were felt to be more stable and susceptible to improving economic development.

The ideology of good governance echoes and elaborates aspects of the modernization theory of the 1960s that held that Western economic and political liberalism represented 'the good society itself in operation'.[10] At the root of both modernization theories and good governance is the Weberian formulation that the world should move toward adopting the features of representative government, a bureaucracy, a capitalist economy, the Protestant ethic and a scientific methodology. The outcome is a disenchanted or secular modern culture. Interestingly, the modern project, which is infused with Weberian undertones, has been largely internalized by policy-makers and thinkers in LDCs and, it permeates even works critical of the postcolonial state in developing countries.

Thus, if the purpose of good governance is the development of modern institutions, such as banking systems modeled on the Bundesbank, it appears to be very similar to the ideology of modernization. One of the drawbacks of both these approaches is that they encourage the notion that only modernity has institutions and that only modernity is rational. Against these presuppositions Sudipta Kaviraj perceptively points out that modernity does not build institutions in an empty space. Rather it reworks the logic of existing structures (Kaviraj, 1991: 72–99). The main difference between good governance and modernization, however, is that while modernization theorists advanced democracy as the outcome of development, growing out of new roads, bridges, rail networks, and television, the new orthodoxy postulates that democracy in its limited form of good governance is a necessary condition of development. Democracy/ good governance is not an aim but the means to attaining a certain stage of development.

The World Bank is thus using the age-old script of the Industrial Revolution in its attempt to forge a New World Order where there will be governance without government. In this system, good governance means in effect less government. Governments would still operate and still be sovereign in a number of ways, but some of their authority would be relocated towards subnational collectivities. Comparing governance and government, Rosenau points to the main differences:

> Both refer to purposive behavior, to goal-oriented activities, to systems of rule; but government suggests activities that are backed by formal authority, by police powers to secure the implementation of duly constituted policies, whereas governance refers to activities backed by shared

goals that may or may not derive from legal and formally prescribed responsibilities and that do not necessarily rely on police powers to overcome defiance and attain compliance (Rosenau, 1992: 3–4).

He sums up governance as 'order plus intentionality'.

Bilateral Aid and Good Governance

An agenda of political conditionality has always been present to one degree or another in superpower dealings with LDCs. In the case of the US, its content had always involved reference to multiparty democracy and human rights. After the breakdown of communism in Eastern Europe, political conditionality was adopted by the European Community Council of Ministers in 1989 and elaborated by the French, British, and German governments the following year. The new agenda contained 'governance issues' as enunciated by the World Bank, with calls for reforms in the sphere of political representation as promoted by the US. Thus these countries did not hesitate to make an explicit linkage between economic and political reforms. Leftwich has quite pointedly demonstrated that the idea of good governance is not simply the new technical answer to the difficult problems of development but an intimate part of the emerging politics of the New World Order (Leftwich, 1993: 613).

In the New World Order, the US's goals for South Asia are quite clearly dominated by a concern for good governance. They are:

> To continue to support and promote security in the region through decreasing tensions between the states: second, to discourage a race toward acquisition of weapons of mass destruction; third, to promote and strengthen democratic institutions through economic development, encouraging privatization and assisting with the buildup of democratic structures; and, finally, to seek support for a successful winding up of the issues raised by the Gulf War.[11]

Sri Lanka can be looked on as a case study of the US approach to development in South Asia. At her senate confirmation hearing in May 1992, Ambassador Teresita Shaffer described the aim of US foreign policy in Sri Lanka as being 'to take advantage of every opportunity to expand US exports or investments' (Human Rights Watch, 1993: 187–88). According to the Sri Lanka desk officer at the State Department, the objectives of US policy towards Sri Lanka are threefold: to encourage a political settlement with the Tamil militants, to foster human rights reforms in the country at large, and to improve economic relations and trade with Sri Lanka, especially in the area of the garment industry.[12]

Sri Lanka governmental sources indicate, however, that human rights are treated only at a general level by the US administration and that the US is satisfied with the steps taken by the Sri Lanka government to improve the nation's human rights record.

The USAID program objectives for Sri Lanka derive from a set of strategic goals that flow from a vision of Sri Lanka as a democratic, environmentally sound, newly industrializing country. It is felt that US assistance can be especially helpful to the Sri Lanka government in managing the transition to a competitive market economy. Both Sri Lanka and the USAID subscribe to the vision of Sri Lanka as a democratic, greener NIC (newly industrialized country). The focus is on agricultural development-led industrialization and private initiative. USAID proposes to broker new private-public partnerships in key development sectors. In this strategic vision, the three following subgoals are defined: an effective market economy; protection of the environment and productive resource base; and an active, pluralistic society. In contrast with its approach in previous decades, USAID has in the 1990s attempted to focus its projects on clear strategic objectives. This was made possible by the conjunction of the Sri Lanka government's economic policy and social objectives with those of the US government. Thus the US continues to promote both political conditionality and good governance as defined by the World Bank.[13]

The European Community has clearly articulated similar concerns in its Resolution on Human Rights in the World and Community Human Rights Policy of 12 March 1993. The Community Policy on 'positive measures and conditionality' asserts that 'the Community can be a very positive force in promoting democracy and human rights, where it has clear international obligations' (*Human Rights Law Journal*,

14(7–8) 1993: 286). Unlike the US approach, though, there is no linkage made between market-friendly policies and human rights. Economic issues do not enter directly into the frame of reference. In the case of the US, there is an underlying assumption that without a free market, there is no respect for human rights, no democracy, and thus no aid.

Critique of Good Governance

There are two necessary and possible dimensions in a critique of good governance. One is qualitative. The question is whether the good governance policy preached by the World Bank is 'good' in all cases. Is it the only way, and if not, are there better roads to development? Let us take a look then at the kernel of the notion of 'good governance', which is the belief that 'good governance' as defined by the World Bank is an essential condition for development in all societies.

Development and Good Governance

One of the central features of 'good governance' through structural adjustment programs is the gradual withering away of the state as an economic actor at the macro level. The underlying assumption is that development—taken here in its least controversial understanding, as the expression of a nation's growing economic well-being, evidenced by increasing quantity of, distribution of, and people's satisfaction with the national wealth—is caused by good governance. Is the equation that clear?

Interestingly, the structural adjustments prescribed by the World Bank for LDCs face at present strong opposition from the Japanese. This is an important development because Japan is the second largest contributor to the bank after the US. The Japanese had begun complaining about the Bank's aid policies in the early 1990s. They pointed out that Japan, Korea, and Taiwan had developed according to a far different model. The governments of the East Asian 'dragons' worked closely with business to develop strategies for growth. Nationalized banks gave low interest loans and grants to selected industries. Governments restricted foreign investment to maintain control over the direction of economic development. Subsidies were granted to business in exchange for specific performance requirements. Planners placed high priority on becoming competitive through higher productivity rather than through lower wages. It was argued that those countries that have followed the American model have floundered since the 1960s, while Japan, South Korea, Taiwan, Malaysia, Hong Kong, and Thailand grew three times as fast as Latin American and South Asian countries and five times faster than sub-Saharan Africa.

The Japanese challenge touches a vital point—namely, the role of the government in the aid recipient countries. It has prompted many policy-makers to rethink the role of the state in economic activity and particularly in central planning. Alternative models inspired by the Japanese experience, or the Scandinavian welfare state, fundamentally differ from 'good' governance as defined by the World Bank, yet they may be better suited to some specific countries or situations. The argument here is not that democracy and development are incompatible but that the state can play an important role without the regime being as authoritarian as neoliberals suggest.

Sometimes the presupposition that democracy/good governance is a necessary condition for development appears in the very choice of countries studied and compared. Atul Kohli, taking the records of five diverse democracies including India, Malaysia (which hardly qualifies as a democracy), Sri Lanka, Venezuela, and Costa Rica and comparing them with countries that followed authoritarian routes to development, has argued that democracies in the developing world can boast impressive economic records in terms of income distribution, debt management, and even growth rate (Kohli, 1986: 153–82). Might not his conclusions linking democracy and development have been quite different had he chosen as case studies countries such as Japan, South Korea, Taiwan, Hong Kong and Thailand, which do not conform to his criteria of democracy?

The link between democracy and development is complex and cannot be encapsulated in a notion such as good governance. Not surprisingly, the concept of 'good governance' has been subjected to scrutiny by human rights activists in Sri Lanka who have expressed doubt about the concern for 'erecting the kind of juridical structure necessary for the spread of market relations' (Abeysekere, 1992: 28). For a developing country such as

Sri Lanka, there is nevertheless no doubt that the main objective of aid and development policies in the 1990s should be to assist integration into the global mainstream. At the same time, aid and development policies will have to continue to serve their traditional objective of supporting long-term development programs for building infrastructures and financing projects of substantial social benefit, such as investment in rural development, health, nutrition, education, and the alleviation of poverty (Sen Gupta, 1993: 453). Just as there is no clear causal relationship between democracy/good governance and development, the linkage between economic growth and social advancement is not self-evident.

Good Governance as Totalizing Discourse

The second dimension of this critique of good governance is of a more fundamental nature. We must ask ourselves why, when all grand narratives or the totalizing or foundational theorizing of modernity have given rise to so many critical responses, a concept such as 'good governance', so anchored in Western history and tradition could ever have been proposed, or flourish. In an era characterized by the loss of paradigmatic guidelines, the concept of 'good governance' has not remained unchallenged. Social scientists are increasingly stressing the need to get away from oversimplified models. Their works indicate that the main problem of political development theories has been their tendency to conceive of political development in terms of two general dichotomies: modern vs traditional societies, and democratic vs non-democratic political systems. Thinking in terms of dichotomies or binary sets of categories prevents us from realizing that many states encompass within themselves many apparently contradictory characters and structures, for example, development and underdevelopment, democracy and authoritarianism, civilian and military rule at the same time.

The development myth is a powerful one. In its name modernizing elites have shed all sensitivity to indigenous systems of thought, totally cast away during the great 'development decades' of the UN system and the transfer of Western science and technology. This particular aspect has been subjected to serious examination by scholars in the developing countries who have investigated the power of the development myth and the creation of a Republic of Science where capitalism had lost its poetic power to a Baconian-scientific worldview (Nandy, 1990). The concept of 'good governance' falls within the tradition of dichotomizing models, which should be once and for all put aside, while the widely accepted concept of 'democracy' must be submitted to the same scrutiny.

At the level of discourse, there is indeed a tendency to confuse deep democracy, embracing all three components of the motto of the French Revolution and based on a complex, multidimensional array of human rights (political, civil, economic, social, and cultural), with good governance, which is nothing more than political liberalization—that is, a process of political change controlled from the top while the social status quo remains unchanged. Democracy confined to good governance entails a change in the shell, not in the fruit. No change in social relations follows. Formal democracy, where democracy is confined to the level of formal electoral participation, is not sufficient. Instead, a return to the notion of human rights that prioritizes basic social rights, or what is commonly known as second-generation rights of individuals (education, health, and well being) may be more useful in any attempt to build deep or progressive democracy that entails profound social reform rather than formal liberties.

One encouraging trend is that development economists at the UN have today ceased to use a narrow concept of development as growth and have begun to concern themselves with the qualitative improvement of life. This trend is reflected in the concept of 'human development indicators' such as freedom of expression, association and movement, the preservation of human rights, and safeguards against intrusion into individual liberty, as preconditions for development (UNDP, 1993). They accept that 'development must be woven around the people, not people around development' (Human Rights Watch, 1993: 1). A more difficult task will be to convince the financial institutions that sound democratic institutions are not enough and that the benefits must seep down to the people. The incidence of riots directed against the IMF in some countries has shown that democracies cannot be created from outside and that a government which is too evidently dependent on external support is liable to lose legitimacy at home.

Conclusion

To paraphrase Sugata Bose, 'somewhere between Sri Lanka and world capitalism lies an interregional arena of social politics and political economy' (Bose, 1990: 357) molded largely by the politics of aid, concepts of human rights, and ideas of good governance. In this arena, the world financial institutions are hegemonic and have stripped away economic sovereignty. The most important decisions, those concerning the economy, are beyond the control of national power holders. The solution is surely not to delink, but rather if one borrows the Hegelian metaphor, to form a circle of circles delineating areas of sovereignty. The outer circle would be formed by circles touching each other while remaining independent. These would be UN institutions, the World Bank, the IMF, and the European Union (EU) and similar organizations. Inside this circle of circles would be all the sovereign states in perpetual movement and interacting between themselves (Amin, 1990). The role of the UN as the conscience of the world has declined while the economic institutions have acquired supranational powers. One of the main reasons why the UN, the IMF, and the World Bank have not succeeded in reducing conflicts, bringing about peace, and generating equitable world development is that these international organizations were not created with a democratic structure. Another important reason is that the UN, the IMF, and the World Bank do not operate as if they form part of the same system. The World Bank, for instance, does not involve the UN in the elaboration and subsequent implementation of the economic stabilization and structural adjustment programs.

There is a possibility that the UN may play a new role in the formulation of a harmonious, cogent, and integrated approach to human rights and development, that of the watchguard of the powerful institutions that lack sensitivity to the human dimension of development. If a reform of the Security Council takes place and if real efforts are made to eliminate wastage, the UN with its egalitarian premises is the best arena where notions of 'good governance' and 'political conditionality' can be discussed and where the smaller and weaker states could have a voice against the hegemonic tendencies that prevail in the aid regime. One can think of a world government in the spirit of Keynes' national economic stabilization formulation, which takes responsibility for managing the world development through a participative and cooperative method of taking decisions and resolving conflicts (Krishna Kumar, 1993: 822).

In this type of world order, there would be no place for single-track and technicist approaches such as good governance. Instead, lending institutions as well as aid agencies and development programs would be 'mindful' of the social, cultural, and political consequences of their intervention. For such a scenario to take place, the relationship between national governments and international institutions must cease to be a power relationship. Such a change can come from many quarters, but there is reason to believe or at least to hope that as more people grow aware that all states are interdependent in crucial areas such as the environment, arms control, or communication, more civil society initiatives will emerge to push for human rights regimes in their own countries and for a more equitable rate of exchange in international aid and development.

Notes

1. For a lucid account of the notion of 'world responsibility' as a rationale of American foreign policy, see Edward Said (1993: 285–91).
2. The rationale and role of aid have been subject to scrutiny. Critics of aid have emphasized the abuses and damaging effects on the recipient society. Others have argued in favor of aid as a catalyst for development. See for instance Robert Cassen and associates (1986).
3. According to the *Human Development Report 1994* (UNDP 1994: 72–73): 'Aid is not targeted at the poor. Donors send less than one-third of development assistance to the ten most populous countries, which are home to two thirds of the world's poor. As a result of these distortions, the richest 40% of the developing world receives as much aid per capita as the poorest 40%.'
4. Interview with George Lister, Senior Policy Advisor, Human Rights and Humanitarian Affairs Bureau, 4 March 1993.
5. See for instance, Report of the Working Group on Enforced or Involuntary Disappearances (7–18 October 1991), Commission on Human Rights, 48th Session, 8 January 1992.
6. Report of the Canadian Human Rights Mission to Sri Lanka, January 1992, p. 22.
7. Statement of Mr Bradman Weerakoon of Sri Lanka Delegation, Commission on Human Rights, 48th Session, Geneva; Statement

by Ambassador Neville Jayaweera, Delegation of Sri Lanka, 12 February 1992.

8. Some donor countries follow the example set by the UN in delinking development aid and human rights. Japan which is Sri Lanka's principal donor has consistently refused to link aid with human rights. In other cases it is less a question of unwillingness than of inability. South Asian regional organizations (ADB, ASEAN, SAARC) have not elaborated policies to deal with the human rights/development linkage.

9. This section draws from Sunil Bastian (1988: 12–18).

10. See S.M. Lipset (1960: 403). Among the political scientists and sociologists who in the 1950s and 1960s put forward modernization theories one can single out the following: Karl Deutsch (1953), David E. Apter (1965), Daniel Bell (1960), Talcott Parsons (1966).

11. Statement of Teresita Shaffer, Deputy Assistant Secretary of State, Bureau of Near Eastern and South Asian Affairs, 7 March 1991, Hearings before the Sub-Committee on Asian and Pacific Affairs. See also Selig H. Harrison (1992: 103).

12. Conversation with Alison Krupnick, Desk Officer, Sri Lanka Bureau, State Department, 15 March 1993.

13. See Annual Budget Submission, FY 1994, Sri Lanka, USAID, June 1992; Strategic Framework FY 1992–96, Sri Lanka, USAID April 1991; Development in Sri Lanka: A review, Sri Lanka, USAID April 1991; Country Development Strategy Statement FY 1983, Sri Lanka, January 1981.

14. A special institutional link between the UN and the financial institutions was established in 1961 with the formation of a 'Liaison Committee' composed of the secretary general of the UN, the president of the World Bank and the International Development Association and the heads of the predecessors of the UNDP. They were to meet periodically and no less than four times a year to coordinate development activities. The Committee never operated formally due to opposition from the World Bank.

References

Abeysekere, Charles. 1992. 'The Limits of Space: Human Rights and Foreign Aid', *Index on Censorship*, 21(7): 28.

Amin, Samir. 1990. *Delinking: Towards a Polycentric World*. London: Zed Books.

Apter, David E. 1965. *The Politics of Modernization*. Chicago: University of Chicago Press.

Asian Cultural Forum. 1993. *Our Voice. Bangkok NGO Declaration on Human Rights.* Bangkok: Asian Cultural Forum.

Bastian, Sunil. 1988. 'NGOs in Development', *The Thatched Patio*, 18(April): 12–18.

Bell, Daniel. 1960. *The End of Ideology.* Glencoe, Illinois: Free Press.

Bose, Sugata. 1990. 'The World Economy and Regional Economies in South Asia: Some Comments on Linkages', in Sugata Bose (ed.), *South Asia and World Capitalism.* New Delhi: Oxford University Press.

Cassen, Robert and **associates.** 1986. *Does Aid Work?* Oxford: Clarendon Press.

Clad, J.C. and **Roger D. Stone.** 1993–94. 'New Mission for Foreign Aid', *Foreign Affairs*, 72(1): 196–206.

Clapham, Christopher. 1993. 'Democratization in Africa: Obstacles and Prospects', *Third World Quarterly*, 14(3): 423–38.

Damrosh, Lori Fishler. 1993. 'The Civilian Impact of Economic Sanctions', in Lori Fishler Damrosh (ed.), *Enforcing Restraint. Collective Intervention in Internal Conflict*, 275, 291–94. New York: Council on Foreign Relations Press.

Deutsch, Karl. 1953. *Nationalism and Social Communication. An Inquiry into the Foundations of Nationality.* Cambridge Mass.: Harvard University Press.

Forsythe, David P. 1993. *Human Rights and Peace. International and National Dimensions.* Lincoln and London: University of Nebraska Press.

Ghosh, Jayati. 1990. 'The Impact of Integration: India and the World Economy in the 1980s', in Sugata Bose (ed.), *South Asia and World Capitalism.* New Delhi: Oxford University Press.

Gibbon, Peter. 1993. 'The World Bank and the New Politics of Aid', *Pravada*, 2(1): 28–35.

Green, R. Herbold, Kim Hong Pyo, and **D. Tong KaWing.** 1990. 'The Language of Money', *Asian Exchange*, 7(3/4): 14.

Harrison, Selig H. 1992. 'South Asia and the United States: A Chance for a Fresh Start', *Current History* (March).

Human Rights Watch. 1993. *Human Rights Watch World Report.* Washington: Human Rights Watch.

Kaviraj, Sudipta. 1991. 'On State, Society and Discourse in India', in James Manor (ed.), *Rethinking Third World Politics.* New York: Longman.

Kettaneh, Gillian. 1990. Human Rights and the Provision of Development Assistance. Unpublished paper presented at the Conference, South Asia—An Agenda for the Nineties, October 1990, Ahungalle, Sri Lanka.

Kohli, Atul. 1986. 'Democracy and Development', in J.P. Lewis and V. Kallab (eds), *Development Strategies Reconsidered*, pp. 153–82. New Brunswick: Transaction Book.

Krishna Kumar, T. 1993. 'Fund-Bank Policies of Stabilization and Structural Adjustment. A Global and Historical Perspective', *Economic and Political Weekly*, 28(17): 815–23.

Leftwich, Adrian. 1993. 'Governance, Democracy and Development in the Third World', *Third World Quarterly*, 14(3): 605–24.

Lipset, S.M. 1960. *Political Man*. London: Mercury.

Nandy, Ashis (ed.). 1990. *Science, Hegemony and Violence. A Requiem for Modernity*. New Delhi: Oxford University Press.

Orenlichter, Diane F. 1992. 'The United States Commitment to International Human Rights', in Richard Pierre Claude and Burns H. Weston (eds), *Human Rights in the World Community, Issues and Action*. Philadelphia: University of Pennsylvania Press (2nd edn).

Parsons, Talcott. 1966. *Societies: Evolutionary and Comparative Perspectives*. Englewood Cliffs, New Jersey: Prentice Hall.

Rosenau, James N. 1992. 'Governance, Order and Change in World Politics', in James N. Rosenau and Ernst-Otto Czempiel (eds), *Governance without Government: Order and Change in World Politics*. Cambridge: Cambridge University Press.

Said, Edward. 1993. *Culture and Imperialism*. New York: Alfred K. Knoph.

Sen Gupta, Arjun. 1993. 'Aid and Development Policy in the 1990s', *Economic and Political Weekly*, 28(11): 453–64.

Tomasevski, Katharine. 1989. *Development Aid and Human Rights. A Study for the Danish Centre of Human Rights*. New York: St. Martin Press.

Turner, Stansfield. 1991. 'Intelligence for a New World Order', *Foreign Affairs* 70(4) (Fall): 150–67.

United Nations. 1993. *Charter of the United Nations and Statute of the International Court of Justice*. New York: United Nations.

———. 1994. *Human Development Report 1994*. New York: United Nations.

UNDP. 1993. *UNDP Human Development Report: Human Development Indicators*.

———. 1994. *Human Development Report 1994*. New Delhi: Oxford University Press.

World Bank. 1989. *World Bank, Sub-Saharan Africa: From Crisis to Sustainable Growth*. Washington DC: World Bank.

———. 1992. *Governance and Development*. Washington DC: World Bank.

Chapter 3

Partnership in Development and NGOs: A Critique of Donor Conceptions

Northern non-governmental organizations and multilateral aid agencies are involved in shaping development in Sri Lanka in two different ways. Not only have they assigned the local NGO sector a special place in the development arena, they have also articulated the concept of partnership as the foundation for development in the present decade. By encouraging the creation of networks between the state, private sector, and local NGOs, donor agencies are intervening with a purpose and in so doing are fast becoming a new circle of power to be reckoned with.

The last 20 years have seen a rapid growth of indigenous NGOs and an explosion of interest on the part of donors in this sector. The new emphasis on the non-governmental sector reflects the intellectual framework of wider changes in macro-economic policy, privatization and the reduced role of states in all aspects of the economy and in the provision of services. At a time when orthodox models lie in tatters, NGOs are seen as dynamic, privatized alternatives to bloated state bureaucracies and are envisioned as vehicles of development, democracy, and empowerment. In Sri Lanka not only bilateral and multilateral donors but also northern NGOs have found these southern NGOs increasingly attractive. Thus in Sri Lanka, international development NGOs which are operational in the country as well as NGOs which are not operational in the country support the activities of the local NGOs. The role of NGOs in development has been transformed. Originally situated in the periphery of the development community, and often directly opposed to its mainstream, these NGOs are now central to contemporary development discourse and practice.

Another important feature has been the emergence of partnership as a key concept in the development discourse in Sri Lanka. The concept of partnership in development has to a large extent replaced aid in the development discourse. While aid suggested an unequal power relation between the giver and the receiver, partnership initially called for a more egalitarian, generous, and responsible relationship for the purpose of development. Later the concept of partnership acquired a more subtle meaning. Just like the concept of civil society, it was an attempt to articulate the problematic relation between the private and the public, the individual and the social, public ethics and individual interests, individual passions and public concerns. But as the meaning of partnership slipped far beyond a concern for humanizing development cooperation, it was increasingly invoked by multilateral donor agencies that harbored a holistic vision of society which the receiver of aid was encouraged to emulate. In this ideal vision, harmonious relations existed between the state, the private sector and the NGO community all engaged in 'developing' their society into a liberal democratic one under the watchful eye of the donor. Partnership was no longer a concept linking donor and receiver but rather linking between them all the different components of the society which received assistance. The meaning of partnership increasingly evolved into one privileging the notion of intersectoral partnership over the notion of North–South cooperation. In this discourse, the NGO sector emerged as a privileged partner of the donor community.

This chapter takes as its primary object not the people to be 'developed' but the apparatus that is to do the 'developing'. It will argue that the donor community is fast becoming a new circle of power in Sri Lanka. The first section will focus on the growth of the local NGO sector in Sri Lanka due to the new emphasis placed upon them by aid agencies and northern NGOs. The second critically examines and compares donor conceptions of partnership in Sri Lanka as politically-oriented discourses. The third section will analyze the obstacles to partnerships evolving and the ideal terrain upon which partnerships can grow. A variety of examples will be taken to suggest the pre-eminently political significance of the notion of partnership as it is articulated by donors. For the purpose of this study, development will be taken as understood in liberal development circles as the expression of a nation's growing economic well-being, evidenced by increasing quantity of, distribution of, and people's satisfaction with the national wealth.

The Emergence of the NGO Sector in Sri Lanka

In the last 10 years, the expanding role of NGOs has drawn comment from international scholars and practitioners.[1] Recently this has included critical studies of accountability and performance in NGO networks. NGOs have become a serious topic of study by anthropologists and sociologists as well.[2] Among the recent works special mention must be made of James Ferguson's case study of the way in which ideas about development are generated and put to use within the context of development agencies in Lesotho (Ferguson, 1994).

In Sri Lanka, there is still very little serious and non-partisan work that has dealt with the non-governmental sector and the development apparatus. Currently no study exists that has empirically examined the impact of NGOs as a whole in Sri Lanka although evaluations of the activities of specific NGOs are often required by funders but not available to the public. The general public is aware of the existence of NGOs as popular newspapers, riding the wave of passé dependency theories, often carry articles critical of the sector that identify it as a fifth column spreading the word of the World Bank, the IMF, or world capitalism. Another type of literature comes from research NGOs specialized in human rights and social sciences which attempts to explain the special role of NGOs in the context of an oppressive state. Often apologetic, these works belong to the genre of works of advocacy by insiders or sympathetic outsiders. At their best they see development agencies and NGOs as part of a great collective effort to fight poverty, promote democratic values, and denounce state excesses. At the worst, they fail to engage in a self-critical reflection and take as a given their moral superiority over the other sectors. They tend to generalize in spite of the lack of data available and envision the NGO sector in Sri Lanka as a homogenous sector which can only have the benefits 'generally' found in other countries. The specificity of Sri Lankan NGOs is rarely addressed:

> They (NGOs) approach their work informally, work from a multidisciplinary perspective, gather information more quickly, and use resources more efficiently, innovatively, flexibly, and in a timely fashion—whether it be human resources, finances, or material goods (Samaraweera, 1997: 9).

Interestingly, the role played by NGOs in the development of the country is not even alluded to in a recent publication examining the 50 years of economic change in Sri Lanka, the word NGO not appearing in the entire book even in the chapter which deals with poverty alleviation (Lakshman, 1997). NGOs are absent, elusive in contrast with their omnipresence in the discourse of the donor community. Their lack of importance seems to be indeed the opinion of mainstream economists, members of the business community and state policy-makers alike in contrast with donor agencies that celebrate the NGOs as the primary agents in their vision of development. A government publication acknowledged, however, that 22 per cent of the total foreign aid received by Sri Lanka was channeled through NGOs.[3]

Internationally, five reasons have been highlighted to explain the growth of the NGO sector. These are increased funding, ideological preferences, program effectiveness and sustainability, external pressure, and the creation of constituencies (Uvin, 1996: 163). In Sri Lanka, specific factors such as the ethnic war must be added as the expansion was driven partly by increased international NGO aid during the political crisis that began in the late 1970s with the emergence of a violent secessionist movement in the north and east of the island.

If one were to describe in a few words the main features of the NGO sector in Sri Lanka, three characteristics need to be highlighted:

- An international NGO sector serving the humanitarian needs of the country stemming from the ethnic conflict.
- A few large and well distributed national NGOs involved in poverty alleviation projects in conjunction with the state or complementary to the state.
- A myriad of small NGOs sometimes called CBOs (community-based organizations) involved in grassroots rural development.

In this chapter, I define an NGO as any association or organization that is non-profit and non-governmental and engaged in relief and rehabilitation, social justice, social welfare, environmental protection, gender equality, development, and human rights. By development NGOs I mean organizations of the NGO sector whose primary concern has been production and distribution of resources and social development.

Histories

Non-governmental organizations have been present in Sri Lanka from the beginning of British rule in the form of local counterparts of organizations affiliated with Christian missionary efforts in the British overseas empire. Located mainly in urban areas, they were most often engaged in social service activities and charity work. The earliest was the Baptist Mission established in 1802. Others, which survive until today, followed it: among them are the Colombo Friend in Need Society (1831) and the Salvation Army (1883). In the latter part of the nineteenth century, as local élites fostered a revival of their respective religions, Buddhist, Hindu, and Muslim non-governmental organizations emerged modeled on their Christian counterparts. The Muslim Education Society (1890), the Maha Bodi Society founded by Anagarika Dharmapala in 1891 and the Young Men's Buddhist Association founded in 1898 were among the first national NGOs although the term NGO was not utilized. This trend continued throughout the last decades of British rule and at the time of Sri Lanka's independence in 1948 there was a sizeable number of NGOs that were involved in social welfare and poverty alleviation activities such as the Ceylon Social Service League (1915) and Lanka Mahila Samiti (1930) while others developed more specialized areas of expertise and international links such as the St John Ambulance Association and Brigade (1906), the Rotary Club of Colombo (1929) or the Red Cross Society (1936). Many NGOs had a religious orientation and strove to promote the interests of specific religious groups: the All Ceylon Buddhist Congress (1919) and the Hindu Board of Education (1921) are cases in point. Others undertaking welfare work had emerged in response to the depression of the 1930s and the malaria epidemic of the mid-1930s. The growth of civil society organizations in the 1930s was closely linked to the grant of universal adult franchise in 1931. Indeed from then on, among the élites of the country, there grew a sense of responsibility for the welfare of their countrymen. Although a measure of self-government was given by the Donoughmore Constitution, associations and civil society movements offered an alternative space where the colonial state was unable to dominate. An important moment for NGOs was when following the 1947 Social Services Commission Report, a Department of Social Services was established. The newly independent state provided NGOs such as the Ceylon Red Cross Society (1949) and the Family Planning Association (1953) with grants-in-aid so as to encourage their performance of welfare activities (IRED, 1991a).

From the 1970s, in many other developing countries, human rights advocates, gender activists, developmentalists, and groups of indigenous peoples became more vocal and operational in many settings that were once thought to be the preserve of governments. It is generally believed that the growth of these 'new social movements' strengthened civil society in specific countries and established international networks of associations. As the role of the state was reappraised and alternatives were sought with which to solve problems, these organizations emerged as critical actors, private in form but public in purpose. Arjun Appadurai uses the term postnational social formations to describe these new organizational forms because they are organized around principles of finance, recruitment, communication, and representation that are fundamentally postnational and not just multinational or international. These new forms did not 'rely on the legal, fiscal, environmental, and human organization of the nation state' and were 'more diverse, fluid, ad hoc, more provisional, less coherent, less organized' (Appadurai, 1996: 167–68).

While in most Asian countries, the 1970s were the decade when NGOs witnessed a phenomenal growth, over 65 per cent of the development NGOs in Sri Lanka were established only after 1977. In Sri Lanka, the most inhibiting factor was probably the all encompassing state power of the United Front government (1970–77), a coalition of left wing parties committed to a tightly regulated system which left little room for a civil society to blossom. In the late 1970s, the change of government heralded an era of openness in society and the economy which had a bearing on the growth of non-state organizations. The role of the government during the decade after 1977 remained significant but while it increased its efforts to develop the nation's infrastructure, it reduced its role in regulation, commerce, and production. Its initiatives received the enthusiastic support of the international development community.

Northern NGOs

In this new context, NGOs grew in numbers while their activities too expanded and diversified. The growth of NGO activity can be linked to two consonant processes. On the one hand, northern public interest in development created conditions for enhanced fundraising. On the other, credible southern counterparts that were competent to request funds, execute projects, and provide financial reports began to emerge from within the communities. The protracted civil war in the 1980s and the consequent refugee crisis also witnessed a new phenomenon as the number of international NGOs operating in Sri Lanka increased sharply. Many took unprecedented steps to establish field offices, especially those traditionally operating programs from headquarters offices. This was the case of three principal relief and humanitarian organizations—Médecins sans Frontières, which was established in Sri Lanka in 1986, UNHCR in 1987 and ICRC in 1990. Most international NGOs in Sri Lanka were assigned a critical role by donors in the implementation of relief operations. Not only were their budgets and the scale of their operations increased, their influence in shaping opinion about the ethnic conflict too was consolidated (Wickramasinghe, 1997). NGOs worldwide gained unprecedented ascendancy with the dismantling of the Soviet Union and the end of the Cold War, which enshrined neoliberalism in the economy and politics as the inescapable model. Sri Lanka like many other developing states was compelled to internationalize its economy and state and in this process the burden of poverty alleviation was increasingly placed within the domain and activity of non-governmental organizations. Two factors seem to have contributed towards a reassessment of development cooperation—the reports of human rights abuses in the early 1990s and the continuation of the war in the north-east. Countries like Norway, Sweden, Denmark, the Netherlands, and Canada were under considerable pressure to terminate the aid relationship or to impose political conditionalities to the continuation of assistance. Denmark did suspend aid and has yet not renewed development assistance. Canadà dramatically reduced its aid for government funded programs and redirected these resources to projects on good governance, human rights, gender, peace and reconciliation. Sweden no longer supports large infrastructure projects. Norway devoted most of its aid program to relief and rehabilitation and other efforts to mitigate the consequences of the war and to help in the healing process.

In recent years, the number of international NGOs in Sri Lanka, what John Clark calls northern NGOs in the south has increased, primarily because of the perceived need to address issues arising from the on-going armed conflict between the government and the LTTE (John Clark, cited in Farrington et al., 1993: 7–8). In the 1990s, Sri Lanka was receiving assistance from the following 50 foreign non- and quasi-governmental organizations (IRED, 1991b):

- Asian South Pacific Bureau for Adult Education
- AUSTCARE
- Australian International Development Assistance Bureau
- Canadian International Development Agency

- Care International, Sri Lanka
- Christian Children's Fund Inc.
- Community Aid Abroad
- Directorate of Development Cooperation and Humanitarian Aid
- Finnish International Development Agency (Finnida)
- FORUT
- Foster Parent Plan International
- Friedrich Naumann Stiftung
- Hellen Keller International Inc. (Sri Lanka)
- Helpage, Sri Lanka
- HELVETAS
- Integrated Community Agricultural Development Agency (ICADA)
- Intercooperation (Swiss Organization for Development Cooperation)
- Intermediate Technology Development Group
- International Executive Services Corps
- International Movement ATD Fourth World
- IRED—Development Innovations and Networks
- Japanese International Cooperation Agency (JICA)
- Konrad Adenauer Stiftung
- Mary's Friends Foundation
- Médecins sans Frontières
- National Centre for Development Cooperation
- NORAD (Norwegian Development Cooperation)
- OXFAM
- Palm Foundation
- Peace Corps, Sri Lanka
- Plan International (Kandy)
- Plenty Canada
- Project SMED (Small and Medium Enterprises Developers)
- RAFAD—Research and Application for Alternative Development
- Save the Children—Red Barna Sri Lanka
- SOS Children's Villages of Sri Lanka
- Save the Children Fund (UK)
- South Asian Partnership
- Sri Lanka Canada Development Fund

- Swedish International Development Agency (SIDA)
- Swedish Organization of the Handicapped
- International Aid Foundation
- Terre des Hommes (Netherlands)
- Terre des Hommes (Suisse)
- The Asia Foundation
- United Nations Children's Fund (UNICEF)
- United Nations Volunteers Domestic Development Services Programme (UNV-DDS)
- United States Agency for International Aid (USAID)
- Voluntary Service Overseas (VSO)
- World University Services of Canada
- World Vision Lanka

This list is a daily reflection of the swarm of expatriate experts who reside and work in the city of Colombo in what is known as the development industry. Among the 50, 39 were created after 1970. Today, a few more must be added. The Ministry of Plan Implementation has signed bilateral accords with 58 international NGOs.[4] They form what is now commonly referred to as a 'global civil society'. This term is used as a loose umbrella term encompassing the domain of 'state sovereignty free' actors with transnational scope who dream of expanding freedom through voluntary association in both domestic and global affairs (Kamal Pasha, 1996: 635–56).

A recent publication differentiated between local counterparts of international NGOs such as the Sri Lanka Red Cross Society, and 'purely Sri Lankan organizations' (Samaraweera, 1997: 7). This division which rests on the assumption that international and national NGOs differ in their structure and organization is not correct. Indeed national NGOs are never totally national in that they are generally heavily dependent on international funding. Furthermore, the structure of a 'national' NGO and its organization depend sometimes more on the type of projects it is involved in than on its affiliation to an international NGO. A far more significant distinction is that between grassroots organizations, which are membership organizations, found at the village level or neighborhood level and NGOs that are grassroots support organizations that seek to create and strengthen membership organizations. Grassroots support organizations may become very large over time, employing hundreds of staff and touching millions of people—this is the case with Sarvodaya Shramadana—but most of them remain small ventures with fewer than 20 employees. Their budgets are small and they depend heavily on foreign aid. Grassroots organizations such as the Maranadhara Samiti or Kulangana Samiti come into being through the activities of grassroots support organizations or foreign aid projects, through imitating neighboring villagers' actions or through internal learning processes. They are composed of farmers, fishermen, women, neighbors, informal sector workers, youth, etc. Their size ranges from a handful of villagers to federated structures composed of thousands of people. Their budgets are small and hard to measure for they largely depend on internally mobilized resources that are difficult to quantify: the time and energy of their members, the labor of volunteers, the financial contributions of villagers, the small savings of women and the materials of artisans. This is the picture at the grassroots: thousands of small organizations with extremely limited budgets apart from the internal resources of their members, and more or less supported by organizations that are small, localized, underfunded and often inefficient and élite based. This picture is corroborated by the data about NGOs, which comes from 293 national development NGOs listed in *Development NGOs of Sri Lanka. A Directory* (IRED, 1991a): there appears to be a predominance of small membership organizations such as organizations of the disabled, fishermen, estate workers or cooperatives involved in social service or rural development. Half of these NGOs claim to be islandwide.

The actual number of NGOs cannot be determined with certainty due to the lack of available documentation and the difficulty in assessing the small grassroots organizations. A recent article suggested the figure of 20,000 (Stirrat, 1997) in 1997 while a 1993 government report estimated that about 25,000–30,000 grassroots organizations were operating in Sri Lanka (NGO Commission Report: 72). USAID's even higher estimate of 50,000 NGOs and CBOs in Sri Lanka seems a little exaggerated (USAID, 1997: 87–112). What is certain is that a statistical mechanism has yet to be devised to classify the different types of NGOs and estimate their number in an accurate manner. Today only approximately 4,000 NGOs are registered with the Ministry of Social Services. The same uncertainty governs estimates at NGO funding. The donor funding channeled to local NGOs has certainly increased if one were to judge it by the expansion of the number of organizations that call themselves NGOs and the emergence of several large organizations employing more than 5,000 people. But the uncertainty about the exact number of NGOs makes it difficult to ascertain the volume of funds they now handle.

Legal Regime of NGOs

Currently Sri Lanka does not possess specific statutory or regulatory provisions that subject NGOs to legal scrutiny. The only mandatory requirements concern voluntary social service organizations, which are required to register with the Ministry of Social Services under the VSSO Act No. 31 of 1980. The VSSO Act originated as an effort to closely regulate NGOs in the social service sector after allegations of malpractices and illegal activities were made against the All Ceylon Buddhist Women's Congress. While the registration of voluntary social service organizations, defined as social service NGOs that are dependent upon public contributions or government grants for funding, is compulsory there are no penalties for those who fail to comply. However only registered organizations are eligible to obtain government grants-in-aid and visas for expatriate staff. The Sri Lanka Red Cross or Helpage fall under this category. The registration of organizations under the VSSO Act was transferred from the Central Ministry of Social Services to the provincial ministries. This was the direct outcome of the ratification of the Thirteenth Amendment to the 1978 Constitution in 1987 and the enactment of the Provincial Council Act No. 42 of 1987. The other statutory schemes for NGOs that do not receive grants-in-aid from the state are: to register as mutual provident societies under the Mutual Provident Societies Act No. 55 of 1949; to be incorporated as limited liability companies under Act No. 17 of 1982 (for example: Law and Society Trust); to be established as trusts under the Trust Ordinance Act No. 9 of 1917; to be registered as 'charities' under the Inland Revenue Act No. 28 of 1979 or as 'approved charities' under the Inland Revenue Act No. 4 of 1965 and lastly by incorporation by an Act of Parliament (for example: Sri Lanka Historical Association).

Government–NGO relations in Sri Lanka have gone through various contrasting stages: relative indifference until the 1970s, ambivalence in the 1980s, and open confrontation in the early 1990s. In the 1980s the state made on three separate occasions attempts to act against NGOs by imposing a stricter supervision. In 1990, after a high powered committee was appointed to investigate allegations that foreign funds were flowing into both international and national NGOs without the knowledge or concurrence of the government, a presidential commission—the Commission of Inquiry in Respect of Non-Governmental Organizations—was formed to conduct a public inquiry. It is generally thought that President Premadasa was motivated by his personal animosity towards the leader of Sarvodaya—an NGO. Indeed, the Commission targeted three NGOs, Sarvodaya, the Eye Donation Society and World Vision. The Report of the Commission issued on 13 December 1993 affirmed the validity of several allegations including unfair and deceitful conversion to Christianity by certain NGOs, malpractices and misappropriation of funds by NGO staff.

'The political role advocated for NGOs at its most innocuous level may be seen as an attempt to influence politics by politicizing development and welfare work even such as health, education and environment, natural resources and technology' (NGO Commission Report, 1993: 139).

President D.B. Wijetunga acted on the NGO Commission's recommendations by the promulgation on 24 December 1993 of an emergency regulation entitled 'The Monitoring of Receipts and Disbursements of Non-Governmental Organizations Regulation No. 1.' Under this regulation, NGOs were defined as non-governmental organizations that are dependent upon the public or government grants-in-aid for funds and that are engaged in social welfare, development, empowerment, research, and environmental protection activities. Cooperative societies and NGOs with annual budgets less than Rs 50,000 were excluded. The regulation required an NGO to register with the director of social services and submit detailed information regarding receipts and disbursements. Heavy penalties for non-compliance were meted into the regulation. NGOs complied with the regulation until the government allowed it to lapse the following year. The general analysis of the NGO Commission episode has been a condemnation of the state's use of emergency measures to unleash its resources against institutions of civil society.

While the distinction between northern and southern, membership and non-membership is a useful one, the distinction made by Clark concerning the orientation of the NGO as 'profit or value ridden' and the approach as being either 'top-down or participatory' is insufficient to describe the complexity of the NGO sector in Sri Lanka. Many NGOs today straddle different spheres of activity: they are both profit motivated and value ridden. The example of micro-finance schemes run by Sarvodaya reflects this dual identity. In the same way, NGOs which act as dispensers of funds to smaller NGOs often combine an attitude of classical top–down enlightened approach in the formulation of a project with participatory methods in the implementation of the project. The landscape of NGOs in Sri Lanka is one where multiplicity is the norm.

The Orderly World of Partnership: Cooperation, Responsibility, and Ideal World

After being for long the preserve of naïve practitioners, participatory development in South Asia has been studied recently in a critical manner by social scientists (Bastian, 1996) but partnership in development remains an untouched area of study except for Sunil and Nicola Bastian's edited volume (Bastian and Bastian, 1997) and R.L. Stirrat's incisive comments in an unpublished essay (Stirrat and Henkel, 1997).

This section will look at the orderly field of statements produced by the 'development' apparatus in order to explore how partnership is justified and practiced. Indeed, as Ferguson has persuasively demonstrated, the thoughts and actions of development bureaucrats are powerfully shaped by the world of acceptable statements and utterances within which they live. Their actions are a product not only of the interests of various nations, classes, or international agencies, but also, and at the same time, of a working out of this complex structure of knowledge (Ferguson, 1994: 18). This section is based on a study of policy documents issued by donors on the issue of partnership as well as on in-depth interviews. Often their official policy on partnership is a patchwork of statements in various documents. One of the keys to understanding partnership is the notion of participatory development. In many ways partnership as a discourse stems from participation.

Participation

Participatory development has been described as the new buzz word of development theory in the 1990s. Describing this new ideal, R.L. Stirrat speaks of a new orthodoxy in the development industry characterized by an approach emphasizing indigenous knowledge and bottom–up planning. The cultural diversity of societies and the pernicious effects of modernization are acknowledged in participatory development. One of the important features of participation as an ideology, apart from its stress on empowerment, on the marginal, on local knowledge, and a bottom–up approach is its distrust of the state. The state indeed fails to empower the people by constantly advocating and practicing a top–down approach to development. Participatory development privileges non-governmental organizations or private voluntary organizations, as they are considered more efficient than state bodies and already embodying the virtues of participation (Stirrat, 1997: 67–92).

Stirrat has analyzed the diverse meanings of the term participation besides its general meaning of taking or being part of something. The concept of participation must be understood in conjunction with the idea of civil society. In the eighteenth century it referred to a realm of social mutuality, in the nineteenth century it was used to characterize that aspect of social existence which existed beyond the realm of the state. One of its genealogies can be traced to the eighteenth century when participation was claimed as a universal principle and civil right. The right of participation in the discussion of public affairs is then a major principle of the enlightenment vision of civil society because it is built on reason itself. Another important genealogy is the Protestant Church's requirement for a good Christian to 'participate' in the liturgy, in governing the Church, and reading the scriptures. Thus the concept of participation is rooted in a specific political tradition and has distinct religious overtones. Stirrat argues that participatory approaches to development far from making a radical shift away from a search for an ethnocentric concept of modernity, are intimately part of the process of modernization. Participatory approaches are means through which people are trained and equipped to become part of the modern world. The difference between this approach and the top–down approach is that instead of forcing the people to modernize, they encourage people to participate in their own 'embroilment in that world'. One of the important features of this approach is the manner in which the donor agency divests responsibility from the agency of development to the participating people. The outcome of the projects is hence not in the hands of the development workers (Stirrat and Henkel, 1997).

Partnership Ideology: The Drift Away From North–South Cooperation

While participation as a concept can be traced to religious roots, partnership belongs to the language of business, sports, and leisure where conflict is non-violent and is normally accommodated through the existence of rules/codes and clearly defined bonds. In the business world, a partnership is a form of business enterprise together with sole proprietorship and corporation. Partnership refers to the realm of market relations and entrepreneurship and is a term that appears to engage closely with the industrialized and globalized world.

The concept of partnership in development can be traced back to the Lomé Convention of 1975. Under a series of agreements known collectively as the Lomé Convention, negotiated between 1975 and 1989, practically all products originating in 69 African, Caribbean, and Pacific (ACP) countries received tariff-free access to the EU market. The idea was to foster a new cooperative relationship between the EU and the developing world. The Swedish International Development Agency (SIDA), that plans and implements the Swedish development cooperation program, lays claim to first using the concept of partnership in the world of aid in its policy paper entitled

'Partnership Africa'. For SIDA, development is conceived as 'a joint responsibility' (SIDA, 1996) (Conversation with Tolvard Akkeson, chargé d'affaires, SIDA, Sri Lanka). Partnership involves a new quality in a relationship in which a fundamentally unequal form of cooperation, aid, will play an important role in the time to come. The term partnership denotes an endeavor to establish a more equal and respectful relationship between the donor and the receiver. Thus at its outset, partnership was conceived as an improved version of cooperation which involved a donor, in this case SIDA, and a receiver, in this case Africa, evolving a new relationship based on jointly discussed values. The issue of the identity of the partners was not decreed in an authoritative way. The question was posed as possible alternatives: Two governments? Two NGOs collaborating with each other? Two companies that implement a joint investment or conclude a deal? Rather than defining the partners, SIDA set out the conditionality of cooperation, which involved shared values, conditions of Swedish support, and a code of conduct for Sweden.

Partnership was initially conceived as a new form of cooperation between donor and receiver founded on mutual responsibility. A fundamental slippage occurred when donors began to advise on building partnerships in society rather than forge partnerships between themselves and receiving communities. From then on donors acquired a feature of *deus ex machina* pulling the strings, forging an ideal world based on their own values.

Partnership as Mutual Responsibility

For most donors, which like SIDA come from a tradition of social democracy, partnership combines the idea of a more egalitarian North–South linkage with the all-encompassing vision of a partnership society. It is a search for a new model of social order characterized by both a reworking of existing international traditions and a search for new ground. It strives to harmonize the conflicting demands of industrial interest and social good.

NORAD, the Norwegian Development Cooperation that is responsible for the administration of Norway's bilateral cooperation with developing countries changed its policy in 1991 'from assistance for which needs and contribution were largely defined in Norway to cooperation in which the recipients are increasingly taking responsibility for defining their own priorities, planning and implementation'. Today, the concept revolves around the notion of responsibility on the part of all parties involved. NORAD works with a variety of partners but does not pose as a precondition that sectors should work together for more effective development. It has a number of bilateral partnerships with the government, namely, integrated rural development in Hambantota and in Moneragala, in the plantation sector and with the Ministry of Justice and Constitutional Affairs. It also has partnerships with large NGOs such as Sarvodaya and grassroots level CBOs. Furthermore, NORAD stresses the differences in approach between local NGOs and the private sector: when NGOs run a business 'it's like government' They are weak in their planning and in their management abilities. More than intersectoral partnership in projects what NORAD sees as essential is the state divesting some of its responsibilities to the NGOs and private sector, for instance on small irrigation projects.[5]

The Canadian International Development Agency (CIDA) was established to enable Canadian missions to finance small development projects in the developing world. The Canadian Fund is its main donor organization and was established in 1973. In Sri Lanka, 50 such projects dealing with farmers, rural population or refugees are funded each year. CIDA has been working with NGOs since 1991. For CIDA the partner is the receiver of the grant: 'Nothing can really be accomplished in development unless the idea comes from partners. Giving the money is easy, compared to what they do with it'. CIDA just like NORAD does not use partnership as a means to reshape the society it is acting upon. Partnership in development signifies a new responsibility for the receiver of aid. The example of a small project at Madawachiya was cited as a positive case of partnership building between funder, project designer, and receiver:

> Four schoolteachers got together and approached the aid officer at CIDA and asked for funds to build 100 toilets. They were first rejected. Then they cut it down to 50 and resubmitted. Once again they were asked to make 25. They agreed. Teachers thus implemented the project. The beneficiaries had to do everything. Collect sand, bricks etc.... Not only did they make 25 toilets but 5 extra ones for that same cost.[6]

In 1992, the vice-president, Canadian Partnership Branch of CIDA drew a contrast between the traditional approach to development, which he called the 'Newtonian universe' in which all development efforts are focused on the state to the current 'Einsteinian era' in which non-governmental groups, both for profit and non-profit are seen as central. His definition of civil society as a sphere morally superior and autonomous from the state includes micro-enterprises, credit associations, private corporations, bankers' associations, universities, professional associations, cooperatives, trade unions, urban popular movements, and rural peasant movements (MacDonald, 1994: 270). What appears quite clearly in this statement is that the state is not part of the circle of privileged partners.

Non-government funders such as OXFAM, Forut, NOVIB and Church-linked organizations such as Christian Aid and World Vision share with the social democratic countries a similar vision of partnership in development.

The Asian Development Bank (ADB) and JICA on the contrary see the developmental state as their partner par excellence. Indeed in Japan, the most important contributing member state of the ADB, the government has always worked closely with business interests to develop strategies of growth. The same sort of analysis is apparent when it comes to aid recipients. The ADB, a multilateral development finance institution created to promote the social and economic progress of the Asian and Pacific region, gives a much lesser role to NGOs in development. Their privileged partners are government institutions, government-owned entities such as the Ceylon Electricity Board, implementation agencies, and provincial governments. Only on very specific projects that need to be implemented in the rural areas are local NGOs used. A local NGO called Sanasa has, for instance, been used as an intermediary.[7] The ADB, unlike the World Bank and UNDP, is more a bank than a political instrument which is trying to bring into being through the collective enterprise of development 'ideal worlds' (Ferguson, 1994: 10). Its main function has been to extend loans and equity investments for economic and social development, to provide technical assistance for the preparation of development projects and to promote and facilitate investment of public and private capital for development purposes. In many ways it resembles a private sector organization.

Stirrat points out that today almost all 'respectable' NGOs still represent their activities in terms of 'partnership' without actually thinking deeply about this ambiguous concept. Partnership, as we have seen, tends to suggest a dilution of individual identity between the said partners by permitting donor NGOs to identify with the developing world and claim a certain authenticity. But while partnership ideology sometimes helps conceptual integration of agendas of funders and NGOs (Stirrat, 1997), in other cases what is articulated is a form of partnership in development which divests responsibility from the donor country or agency to the receiving party. The most crucial departure from the notion of partnership as North–South cooperation can be seen in the interventionist attitude of some funders who by calling for intersectoral partnership of a particular type are in effect attempting to transform or at least order the society they are providing development funds for.

Partnership as Social Transformation

The United States Agency for International Development (USAID), the foreign aid arm of the US government offers a strong contrast with Japan's indifferent attitude to NGOs in the development process. It gives help on a government to government basis or directly to indigenous private organizations. As USAID has a bilateral agreement with Sri Lanka, priority is given to partners called by the state. Any other project needs the approval of the government. USAID has nevertheless worked with a number of local and international NGOs including CARE, Sarvodaya, Agromart, Friend in Need Society, Terre des Hommes, Community Front for Prevention of Aids for instance. They have funded in the last 10 years around 25 local and international NGOs. The concept of partnership has been quite clearly defined in the New Partnership Initiative (NPI) launched by former US Vice-President Albert Gore. NPI is an integrated approach aimed at 'building partnerships that foster sustainable development among three sets of key actors at the local level—civil society, institutions of democratic governance and the business community' (USAID, 1997). In the NPI there is an idealization of local government, which is considered more democratic than the central government.

In Sri Lanka, the NPI incorporates a definite political agenda which entails 'maintaining political and social stability'. The partners are also clearly defined: 'capable local institutions, such as empowered NGOs, a vibrant small business sector, and effective local government working in partnership with citizens groups'. USAID's understanding of partnership appears to be 'intersectoral partnership' while the purpose of forging such a partnership is not a politically neutral type of development aimed at poverty alleviation but a politically-loaded program: 'The indirect purpose of this and related assistance is to present devolution as a development issue, rather than primarily a political issue' (ibid.: 87–112). The selected partners of USAID are essentialized and vested with intrinsic qualities in a discourse, which begs resemblance with the colonial habit of typifying groups and communities. They are described as 'capable, empowered, vibrant and effective' qualities that may exist but surely not in all institutions.

The World Bank practical guide summarizes the position of the Bank vis-à-vis partnership with NGOs. NGO-Bank collaboration is frequent but in many cases the quality of the interaction is limited to project implementation. With the term partnership, the Bank is looking at 'enhanced roles for NGOs earlier on in the project cycle'. The principal 'partners' of the Bank have been until now, 'borrowing governments and for-profit private sector firms' (World Bank, 1995). 'The shifting development context has led to a move away from strictly bilateral donor-government relationships and towards a greater focus on partnerships between governments, donors and civil society' (World Bank, 1996: 1). Civil society, which the World Bank often conflates with NGO sector, is the third participant in the development trialogue. Partnership is couched in moral categories: '...collaboration with nongovernmental organizations is good for the Bank, the government, and the NGOs. Most importantly, it is good for the people, particularly the poorest people who might not otherwise be reached' (World Bank, n.d.: 2).

The World Bank is today the most articulate and influential promoter of partnership in development. More than any other development agency, the World Bank has selected, adapted, and adopted the NGO participation agenda insofar as it strengthens and promotes local involvement in project management.

But it has resisted a call for participation in national economic policy and resisted the critique of adjustment lending. The World Bank plays a crucial role among donors as the regulator, financier, and coordinator of official aid donors. There is an added significance when one considers the influence of the World Bank among donors and other development practitioners, and its intellectual leadership through publications, training, and collaboration with other donors. The World Bank has successfully moved from being a target of NGO criticism to position itself as a lever, an ally by adopting the language of popular participation. The authority of the Bank to prescribe policy and institutional changes in several fields has been increasingly accepted (Nelson, 1996: 606). Once partnership is internalized by funders it is difficult for NGOs to critique the effects of orthodox adjustment plans on income distribution, public services to the poor, resource depletion, and food self-reliance. In the same way, partnership ideology makes it difficult for state actors who are also involved in this framework to accuse funders of privileging civil society as opposed to the state as in the case of participatory development. The result has been successful to a certain extent as in Sri Lanka there has been no vigorous national debate over adjustment programs or of the World Bank as an agent of 'disciplinary neoliberalism' (Gill, 1995: 399–423).

The UNDP unlike the World Bank sees two different types of partnerships that function simultaneously. There is a recent direct linkage between the UNDP and civil society. UNDP, which works primarily with governments, acknowledges that since the 1980s it has increased its collaboration with civil society organizations at every level. But in so doing, one of UNDP's avowed objective of partnership with civil society is to promote dialogue among governments, civil society, and the private sector to help define policies that support sustainable development. The position of the UNDP is made quite clear by one of its administrators:

> We in UNDP are committed to facilitating the involvement of civil society organizations, including NGOs, through partnerships with governments and the private sector, in promoting people-centered development (UNDP, n.d.: 1).

Partnership is the instrument that has transformed northern NGOs and aid agencies into new circles of power. Indeed by adopting intersectoral partnership instead of participation as the foundation of their developmental vision, multilateral donors are spreading their tentacles to society in its entirety and intervening in its transformation. The decision to privilege NGOs rather than political parties or trade unions as intermediaries between the unorganized masses and the state is a calculated one. Indeed when the World Bank promotes partnerships as project methodology couching it in the language of economic effectiveness rather than of political values, the effect is an inevitable depoliticizing of society.

Tensions or Harmony in Intersectoral Partnerships?

NGOs, the state and the private sector have understood and adapted the prevailing partnership discourse in many different ways. As it leaves the desk of policy-makers and enters the world of practice, the partnership discourse displays its flaws and contradictions but also its potential richness.

Power Relations: Partnership and Cooperation

Most NGOs in Sri Lanka are small grassroots organizations involved in poverty alleviation schemes, rural development and rural credit. Many of their programs seem to be operating in isolation from the rest of the economy, from other agencies and programs in the same field, from government policy and from established networks of production and specialization and sometimes even from the socioeconomic milieu of the community in which they are located.

For NGO staff the language of partnership is irrelevant. What exists instead is a very definite power relationship between the funder and the receiver and the growth of chains of organizations or individuals, which mediate between the donor and the ultimate receiver. A grassroots organization may appeal to a local NGO, which may in turn appeal to its head office in Colombo, which will then apply for support from an international NGO. In this vast network of organizations and consultants devoted to the cause of development, partnership is often traded for patronage, political manipulation, and power games. At a local level, individuals with political aspirations frequently establish their own NGOs and use the resources they have access to and the contacts they make as means of advancing their interests. In Passera, in the Badulla district, one such NGO was born for the principal purpose of promoting the political career of its director at the local level. The director was supported by a radical party. Between a small NGO and a foreign donor the notion of partnership does not make any sense, as there is no direct link between them. The intermediary who masters the language of the funder while sympathizing with the goals of the recipient plays a crucial role. The intermediary is often a member of the Colombo middle-class, Westernized in outlook; human rights, gender, empowerment, governance are issues that he or she is familiar with but is nativist in habits; he or she admires the simple and clean life of the rural folk; who by virtue of a long personal and professional association with the Internation Non-Governmental Organization (INGO) community in the island has their trust. Whoever he or she recommends or sponsors is a worthwhile candidate for aid.

Apart from funding secured by intermediaries one innovative approach to NGO funding was introduced recently by an organization called the Research and Application for Alternative Financing for Development (RAAFD). It provides a credit guarantee to a local bank, which can be used by an NGO to borrow against. If the NGO defaults in the repayment the bank cashes the guarantee. NGOs such as Uvagram and Sarvodaya have used this mechanism with the help of IRED (Alailima, 1995: 1–24). The challenge is, however, to extend such funding opportunities to less well-known NGOs.

With small NGOs there is an undeniable asymmetrical relationship between donor and recipient. The donor has the power to choose his recipient/partner and he will tend to choose a recipient/partner whose aims coincide with his own. Further the receiver is accountable to the donor and not the opposite. If the donor decides to cease funding the receiver has no recourse. In the chain of relationships between donors and receivers partnership is perhaps the least suitable term to describe the nature of the relationship between small NGOs and international donors.

Most practitioners of development have realized the difficulties in forging real and lasting partnerships between the state, the NGO sector, and the private sector. The main difficulty has been the differences in ideology, work ethics, and loyalties, which exist in these three sectors. In general, the efficiency of the NGO sector to implement development projects has also been called into question. While continuing to discharge the task of poverty alleviation to NGOs, funders such as USAID and the World Bank are looking into other options which transcend the public sector–private sector divide. USAID has developed a public–private partnership to manage coastal resources in the south of the country and has encouraged the participation of communities and local government in biodiversity management in Ritigala in the North Central Province. What is significant in these two projects is the institution building process. Indeed in both cases, new institutions emerged with the help of the funding agency. In the Rekawa seaside rural community in the Hambantota, in the absence of a single NGO representing the community, the Rekawa Fishermen's Cooperative Society was encouraged by USAID to bring the wide range of CBOs together and form a single registered NGO: the Rekawa Development Foundation was created to be responsible for representing the community in natural resources management and other decision-making processes. The same process took place in Ritigala where the Tanthirimala Gramodaya Mandalaya was identified as the most capable indigenous institution to facilitate the formation of a 'representative' NGO to manage the Ritigala community-based resources management project: the Ritigala Community Base Development and Environment Foundation (RITICOE) was established in 1995 and is presently headed by two young women 'leaders from the community'.

In this sense, USAID is rationalizing a diffuse civil society and creating institutions, which can collaborate with the local government and central government. There is an interventionist attitude on the part of USAID to foster a more enabling environment for partnerships to blossom. Not only are 'representative' institutions created, leaders of the community are also selected by the funding agency.

State–Private Sector–NGOs:
Strained Partnerships

Donors promoting better state–private sector–NGO relations often articulate their projects in an ideal framework without considering the very specific features of the Sri Lanka state, which could or could not allow such relations to succeed. The Sri Lanka state of the 1990s is an overdeveloped centralized state manned by a bureaucracy which has not been at the forefront of modern thinking. The NGO and private sector personnel too have different approaches which bear on their relations. While some smaller NGO personnel have a 'public sector mentality' which values popular and indigenous knowledge rather than modern approaches, the private sector personnel are totally cut away from the other sectors as far as work ethic, corporate culture, and ideal worlds are concerned.

Even between the private sector and state policy-makers, partnerships are beset by practical difficulties although both have in common the belief that market and growth lead to happiness. The Sri Lankan state understands development as integration into the national and international capitalist markets. In the minds of most decisionmakers it has become increasingly evident that the market should no longer be viewed as an institution which must be regulated by external social forces but on the contrary that it should be used to regulate society as a whole. In Sri Lanka, the government has given the private sector a lead role in the financing and operation of physical infrastructure such as transport, energy, and telecommunications, with the state stepping back to assume a regulatory stance. Social infrastructure, on the other hand, tends to be seen in large measure as the preserve of the state because of the inherent market failures associated with the provision of public goods such as health and education.

A good example of partnership between the state and the private sector for infrastructure development is Private Sector Infrastructure Development Company (PSIDC), a public company where the majority shares are held by the government. This company provides long-term subordinated debt for private sector infrastructure projects (World Bank, 1996). In that sense it is a partnership between the donor, in this case the World Bank that approved the loan to set it up, the state, and the private sector. In spirit, PSIDC is neither private, nor public. As a development fund its profits are reinvested in the fund and its purpose is social service on a large scale. The question addressed here is whether this type of organization constitutes for donors the future of development: Is development going to create a new type of organization, which is small and efficient as some NGOs, apolitical as private sector institutions, not driven by profit like NGOs but striving for the good of the community like the state? Recent data tends to suggest that PSIDC is facing difficulties due to the state bureaucracy's stranglehold. Indeed two years after its creation no development project has left the paper stage.

The State and NGOs

There have been very few studies assessing the relationship between the state and NGOs. While Abeywardena's study dealt with a situation which preceded the 1990–93 confrontation between state and NGOs (Abeywardena, 1989) and Alailima analyzed in a technical manner the range of mechanisms currently operating in the Asian region to engender cooperation between governments and NGOs in the planning and implementation of development activities (Alailima, 1996: 1–26), a more recent study by the Law and Society Trust (LST) has not gone beyond reiterating data from the NGO Commission Report (Samaraweera, 1997). The post-1993 period is yet to be seriously scrutinized. The relationship between the state and NGOs is certainly less conflictual than the Sinhala nationalist press and politically radical NGOs would like to suggest (for more details see Chapter 4, this volume). Open conflicts, in fact, rarely arise between the state and NGOs involved in rural and technical development—except when they arouse the jealousy of statesmen as in the case of Sarvodaya—but between the state and human rights NGOs who purport to act as watchdogs of state excesses. Even the NGO Commission which was the most forceful attempt at deafending the voice of NGOs acknowledged the role NGOs could play in poverty alleviation while offering a sound warning to others:

For example human rights issues should not be used as political issues for confrontation with the government but as pure human rights issues (NGO Commission Report: 52).

The relationship between state and NGOs involved in development has been and is today one of timid experimentation. The earliest recognition of an NGO role is seen in the Children and Young Persons Ordinance of 1939 and the Orphanages Ordinance of 1941, which empowered government agencies to obtain the services of NGOs in the rehabilitation of young offenders. Further evidence of government recognition came in the Freedom from Hunger Campaign of 1960. NGOs were represented on its committee and NGOs such as National Heritage, Nation Builders Association and National Development Foundation worked with the state on the promotion of minor irrigation schemes. The Gramodaya Mandalayas established under the Development Council (Amendment) Act of 1981 provided for the participation of NGOs in local level planning and implementation. Later NGOs participated and collaborated with more or less success in government lead projects such as the Gam Udawa, Integral Rural Development Program and Mahaweli Development Project (Abeywardena, 1989: 49–56). In the post-1977 period, NGOs collaborated with the government on programs related to children and women. Although the role played by development NGOs in grassroots development was acknowledged— the Janasaviya Implementation Guidelines considered NGOs as 'essential and integral partners in the program' (ibid.: 39)— the nature and the sustainability of the institutional cooperation between the state and the NGO sector have not been sufficiently analyzed. What is the situation today? Under the National Environmental Act, seven NGO representatives sit on the Environmental Council which advises the Central Environmental Authority while the NGO Panel in the Women's Bureau and the NGO Committee of the Children's Secretariat created during the previous regime are now defunct. The NGO liaison unit in the Ministry of Policy Planning and Implementation also created during the UNP regime remains active although without a formal status. According to an official in the Ministry of Planning the NGO liaison unit is not a formal body although it has been allocated the task of dealing with foreign NGOs.

The most important function of the NGO liaison unit has been to negotiate memoranda of understanding (MoU) with international NGOs engaged in Sri Lanka (NGO Commission Report: 49–50), although this unit was allegedly established to facilitate and assist NGOs in various activities. In 1993, of 47 international NGOs reported to be operating in Sri Lanka, 40 appear to have signed an MoU (Samaraweera, 1997). Five years later there were 58 signatories with the Ministry of Plan Implementation and a few others with other ministries. Other MoUs were signed with other ministries such as the MoUs between the Red Crescent Society and the Ministry of Social Services or between the VSO and External Resources.[8] An MoU provides for instance for the ministry to be responsible for providing facilities to NGOs such as recommendations for issue of visas, recommendation for exemption of customs duty on imports of equipment, etc. The MoU is not a stringent instrument since it is not imperative for an international NGO to sign an MoU in order to enter the country. If a well-known local NGO such as Sarvodaya invites a foreign NGO to collaborate on a project with the concurrence of the secretary, Ministry of Social Services, no MoU is necessary.

Apart from the Environmental Council, the National Commission on Disabled and the National Monitoring Committee on Child Rights which have NGO representatives, the existence of an NGO liaison unit for foreign NGOs to sign MoUs and an NGO secretariat for local NGOs to register, the state does not formally acknowledge a special role for NGOs in the development of the country. What most studies of NGO–state relations do not sufficiently emphasize is that the dismal number of state–NGO partnerships is enough to prove the lack of understanding that governs relations between these sectors. Indeed if there was really a concerted effort to involve NGOs in the development effort of the state, formalized collaborations in so many other fields such as agriculture, rural development, education, and health would have taken place. The reluctance to work together is of course mutual. NGOs too are reticent towards state involvement that they see as interference and confidence-building measures on the part of the state have yet to be imagined.

Collaboration on Poverty Alleviation Projects between State and NGOs: Instrumental Partnership

Despite explicit willingness on both sides, cooperation between NGOs and government agencies is limited and mainly takes place at the local level on poverty alleviation projects. For the state quite clearly partnership with NGOs does not grow naturally out of its developmental vision. It is more a means to achieving certain objectives.

In 1988–89, the electoral victory was achieved partly by incorporating within the package of structural adjustment policies (SAP) an electoral commitment to an extensive 'safety net' program in the form of a large income transfer scheme for the declared purpose of 'poverty alleviation'. This program was later referred to as the janasaviya program (Lakshman, 1997: 10). A National Development Trust Fund formerly called the Janasaviya Trust Fund (JTF) was set up in May 1991 to implement the Poverty Alleviation Project sponsored by the World Bank. The JTF was what is generally called a Socio-Economic Development Fund and was jointly funded by the government and bilateral or multilateral donors. Development funds are multisectoral and involve NGOs as intermediaries to implement sub-projects in a more flexible way. Although they constitute a good example of partnership in the funding mechanism between state and donors in the case of the JTF, the state–NGO partnership was a failure. The Sri Lanka government at that time had acknowledged the need for NGO participation in the implementation of the project. But NGO–state relations were seriously undermined by the investigations of the NGO Commission and by the lack of autonomy of the fund vis-à-vis the government. Many of the country's NGOs including Sarvodaya chose not to participate in the disbursement of funds. With the election of the new government in late 1994 changes were introduced in the management and this resulted in new areas of collaboration between the fund and NGOs (Malena, 1997).

A recent study has described the links that have been established between NGOs and government agencies and programs as 'superficial and tenuous', the exception being the Small Fishers' Federation working relationship with the North–Western

Provincial Council. CARE has not succeeded in the same manner in spite of efforts being made in that direction. The same study has indicated that the government is particularly ill-suited to implementing bottom–up poverty alleviation strategies, owing to a lack of skills and the avenues that open up to political patronage. 'Many government led programs revert to top down approaches sooner or later' (Gunatilaka, 1997: 54–55). Thus partnership is not a natural way of working for state institutions. In so doing they go against their natural propensity to a top–down approach to development and the mitigated results demonstrate the forced nature of such collaborations.

The Private Sector and NGOs in Microfinance: Partnerships or Mirror Images?

The World Bank declared quite definitely in 1975 that 'rural development is concerned with the modernization and monetization of rural society, and with its transition from traditional isolation to integration with the national economy' (Ferguson, 1994: 260). It is then quite logical that in this vision the banking sector should be encouraged to play an important part in the development process. In this spirit the World Bank in the 1990s promoted the smaller end of the business spectrum, what is generally known as microenterprise. On paper microenterprise accounts for almost half of the workforce but in reality they do not resemble entrepreneurs. Microenterprise is, in fact, a euphemism for what used to be known as the informal sector, much of which is people eking out an existence, in whatever way they can. Providing credit for the poor has been advanced as a powerful weapon against poverty. But there are many obstacles for such schemes to succeed: on the one hand, private sector involvement is limited by the consideration that microfinance is not generally commercially feasible, and on the other, the public sector has been more preoccupied with the alleviation of poverty through direct hand-outs and political intervention.

In the 1990s, two parallel processes are taking place in the area of microfinance: a new involvement of NGOs in microfinance and NGO-banking sector partnerships in microfinance schemes. One of the consequences of NGO interest in financing schemes has been a significant change in the personality and culture of the NGO. The usage of the term private sector organizations in a recent World Bank Report on Hatton National Bank (Gallardo et al., 1997: 6) for organizations which normally are perceived as belonging to the NGO sector reveals the merging of identities between institutions performing very similar functions. Indeed it cites the following 'private sector organizations' which have 'carried out a significant number of income generating and job-creating programs, funded mostly by financial resources generated on their own initiative and/or supplemented by international donor agencies': Sarvodaya movement, SANASA Thrift and Credit Cooperative Societies, Women's Development Federation of Hambantota District and its Janashakthi Bank Societies, People's Rural Development Association and Hatton National Bank's (HNB) Gami Pubuduwa (GP) program. While the GP program is the only avowedly for profit program and the other organizations do not call themselves financial institutions, they too charge an interest rate on the loans given to recipients.

Sarvodaya Economic Enterprises Development Services (SEEDS) for instance, which is the rural economic program of the Lanka Jathika Sarvodaya Shramadana Sangamaya, was created as a separate division in 1986. Its operations commenced in 1988, initially among 250 Sarvodaya Shramadana Societies in five districts. At the end of 1996, about 2,000 such societies had been formed in 20 districts. The target group of this program is the multitude of rural poor who are members of the Shramadana Societies. SEEDS plans to uplift the economic status of the target groups by inculcating savings habits among them and meeting their small-scale financial requirements. Loans are granted after the members go through a compulsory savings program for at least six months (*Central Bank of Ceylon Annual Report*, 1996: 172). What is interesting is that in its brochure, SEEDS describes itself as 'the leader among Sri Lankan NGOs operating in the field of rural economic development'. Thus SEEDS has a distinct NGO identity. Although the services it provides are very similar to that of the HNB's GP scheme, the significant difference resides in the aims of the project. While the GP scheme's aim is poverty alleviation through the provision of a credit line,

SEEDS has a clear ideological tinge in the microfinance project. Its aim is to promote 'friendly economic development activities' and to encourage 'prevailing life-style and values' (SEEDS, n.d.: 1) and rural development 'through people's participation'. SEEDS unlike the HNB scheme is a scheme anchored to ideals such as participatory development and to a political vision of society as unchanging and non-modern. Among the expectations for the future are 'the lessening of social injustice through gender education' and 'the building up of a national team of specialists competent in alternative development methodologies' (ibid.: 12). The HNB scheme is devoid of a gender component although the question of credit to women as a target group is addressed and its main aim is to finance projects, which can grow into large entrepreneurships. The comparison of these two schemes begs questioning on eventual partnerships between the private sector which has taken as a given a particular understanding of development and does not question its validity and NGOs which are politically motivated institutions.

The Hatton National Bank (HNB), a private bank set up a credit scheme, Gami Pubuduwa (GP) or 'village reawakening' in 1989 to facilitate microenterprise development in a political context of youth unrest. It targeted the poor and has proved financially sustainable. The scheme is operated through the bank's all-island branch network. There are today 64 branches through which the GP units that number 94 are operated. Each branch office has a Gami Pubuduwa Upadeshaka (GPU) who is given six months' training and who works on flexible time, mixing in the community, building up personal relations with potential customers and judging their creditworthiness. He or she is offered special incentives and is limited in the number of loans that can be offered to ensure manageability. GPU is responsible for assessing projects in terms of cost, necessary loan size, and prevailing market conditions and expected profit. The scheme is flexible in collateral requirements and it provides up to Rs 25,000 without collateral. Established and tested entrepreneurs can obtain loans of up to Rs 100,000 without collateral, the interest rate being 16–18 per cent per annum. The scheme is confined to a 15-mile radius from the branch office. The GP scheme is a good example of the relations that exist between the private sector and the NGO sector. There are on the one hand institutional relationships with NGOs engaged in microfinance, Sarvodaya, SANASA and other NGOs through the UNDP-CARE network of microfinance institutions which involves a share of the targeted beneficiaries of loans between the NGOs and the GP. The NGOs address the layer referred to as the laboring poor who are employed full-time in unskilled labor positions and the self-employed poor categories, while the GP program focuses on the upper layers of the poverty pyramid, the self-employed, the entrepreneurial, and the near poor. Thus HNB does not compete with the NGOs. The GP is also taking the experience of SEEDS and Janashakthi village bank societies in group or solidarity lending schemes as models for experiments in solidarity lending. In the spirit of NGO community work the GP is also attempting to create good relations with the community by holding lectures, helping in filling forms, participating in community development by renovating temples. Clearly NGO methodologies are being adapted by the HNB. While Sarvodaya's SEEDS is an NGO that resembles a private sector institution, HNB's GP scheme has drawn from the NGO model of grassroots development. The future may see a further merging of identities and a blurring of boundaries between sectors.

Technology/Modernization: The Favorable Terrain for Partnerships

Intermediate Technology Development Group (ITDG) was founded in the United Kingdom 30 years ago by E.F. Schumacher, the author of *Small is Beautiful*. His idea was to promote a type of technology that could help improve the lives of the large number of people whose needs are often not considered 'development' priorities. ITDG has offices in Bangladesh, Kenya, Peru, Nepal, Sudan, Sri Lanka and Zimbabwe. Their work internationally focuses on the following areas: building and shelter, energy, food processing, agro-processing, manufacturing, transport, mining, disasters and vulnerability.

According to ITDG's policy director, partnership between funders, the organization, and the population, which will benefit from a project is rarely practiced.[9] At the level of formulation of a project there is already a gap, as the community is not involved in the writing of a proposal. What happens in fact is that ITDG projects are formulated keeping in mind their maximum fundability. ITDG was initially set up in Sri Lanka in 1989 with a block grant from ODA, now called the Department for International Development (DFID). DFID wants a focus on the four following issues in any project: livelihoods, environment, gender, and sustainability. Since 1998, funding has been coming more on a project base which means less time for investigatory work. ITDG's situation reflects the vulnerability of NGOs which depend on external funding for their daily running. The funder has the ability to set an agenda and only within this framework is a form of partnership possible. The community, however, is excluded from the decision-making process.

If a partnership between the community and the funder does not take place in practice, the relation between ITDG, the state, and the business community must be emphasized. Through various forums ITDG brings together different sectors involved in the same field. There is, for instance, an Energy Forum and a Transport Forum. The Energy Forum is a discussion group around the theme of alternative energy forms. Officials and individuals from the government, the private sector as well as the NGO sector participates in the seminars. Often these seminars lead to a better understanding between individuals who though from different perspectives are all working in the same field. Ceylon Electricity Board (CEB) attended meetings and gradually personal contacts were strengthened. It built its credibility through work. Frequently CEB professionals work as advisors on ITDG's projects and ITDG professionals participate in CEB projects. Pilot projects may follow as in the case of biogas.

The micro-hydro project on tea estates was implemented with the tea company as partners and the ministry of environment. The components of the turbines were manufactured locally by trainees who can aspire in the future to become successful entrepreneurs. Dhanapala, an ITDG economist, stresses the importance of going in with local authorities for a wider impact and replicability of the project through the government arm in a district. This relationship is important for the sustainability of the project. In Sabaragamuwa local authorities have funded certain small projects and ITDG has provided the technical expertise and assistance.

ITDG also works with the private banking sector and helps viable projects to be funded. Seylan Bank for instance has lent Rs 800,000 for a project by ITDG and Hatton National has financed micro-hydro projects. State rural banks are considered more difficult to work with as they most often deal with the most powerful villager in the community and are reluctant to forge new networks.[10] ITDG's technical request unit or representative works with Sarvodaya, one of the largest NGOs in Sri Lanka to identify the needs of a community. A cycle trailer project was developed in that manner. The Sarvodaya Rural Enterprise Development Service (REDS) and the Cathy Rich Memorial Food Processing Training Unit (CRMFPTU) have played important roles. REDS being an organization with an extension network operating in 21 districts, helps the project disseminate information and in turn provides the project with information on the activities and needs of rural communities. CRMFPTU shares information mainly through its network of trainees. ITDG establishes close links with the community and makes them responsible. In the micro-hydro project for instance, villagers have to pay for their electricity. But they gain a sense of worth as they have succeeded in breaking through their isolation without the help of politicians. The micro-hydro project for instance needed only a 50 per cent grant element.

ITDG and its counterpart AGROMART Foundation, a local NGO which specializes in empowerment of rural marginalized poor are partnership success stories because they combine a number of enabling factors: their staff is small, local, well qualified in technical matters.[11] Their projects are small scale, manageable, and well defined. Their links with funders are assured by a commitment to certain criteria—gender sensitivity, capacity building, sustainability. They are small efficient units which resemble private sector organizations but that are motivated by a desire to transform society giving the poor a better deal. They do not critique or oppose the modernizing nation-state with which they share core values. But they are conscious that there are multiple forms of oppression, which come with the linkages proposed by partnership promoters.

They understand and are able to react to the ways in which old and new elites at the local, the regional, and the national level attempt to retain or gain control over resources. As their staff is from the country they are aware that the predilection of some donors—USAID for instance—for provincial government institutions or district level institutions is based on a false premise that decentralized institutions are less clientelist, nepotistic, and corrupt than the central government. Partnerships in these two cases emerge from the NGO's needs and are not the implementation of policies framed in another hemisphere. That is the reason why to a certain extent they work.

Conclusion

There has been a drive of development from simple goals of poverty alleviation to holistic aims of redesigning the state and society of the country. By adopting partnership as a central principle of development in countries such as Sri Lanka, donors have emerged as important actors in the society and politics of the land. Instead of letting social forces combine and conflict freely, they are taking the dangerous path of attempting to create imagined spaces of harmony. Their role has singularly expanded from funding and project appraisals to a multi-faceted policy that privileges non-governmental involvement in development. By emphasizing their role in the development of the country, donors are making sure that the constituency, which initially refused SAP, will collaborate. By promoting participatory development they are winning the NGOs to their side while focusing most of their attention and funds in state and private sector large-scale development under the SAP. NGO development in Sri Lanka is best described as an appendage to the market-oriented growth. The ultimate goal is to ensure that social order prevails.

Notes

1. See John Clark (1994), Julie Fisher (1993).
2. See the Annotated Bibliography in Thomas G. Weiss and Leon Gordenker (1996: 227–40).

3. See, Report of the Presidential Commission of Inquiry in Respect of Non-Governmental Organizations Functioning in Sri Lanka (13 December 1993) (unofficially released version) (cited as: NGO Commission Report), p. 68.
4. Communication with Mr Halwatura, Assistant Director, Ministry of Plan Implementation and Parliamentary Affairs.
5. Communication with Mr Leelasena, Senior Advisor Development Cooperation, NORAD, Sri Lanka.
6. Communication with Ms Marnie Garvin, Councelor Development, and Aloy Perera, Development Officer, CIDA, Colombo.
7. Communication with T. Kondo, Resident Representative and K. Tilakaratna, Implementation/Program Officer, Asian Development Bank, Colombo.
8. Communication with Mr Halwatura, Assistant Director, Ministry of Plan Implementation and Parliamentary Affairs.
9. Communication with Vishaka Hidellage, Policy Director, ITDG.
10. Communication with K. Dhanapala, Economist, ITDG.
11. Communication with Ms Beulah Moonesinghe, Chairperson Agromart Foundation. This NGO formed in 1990 has today a staff of 110 members and a budget of Rs 36 million annually. The projects focus on the following areas: entrepreneurship training; economic literacy training; vocational training; leadership training; political empowerment training; trade fairs/marketing; revolving loan scheme; information and data collection.

References

Abeywardena, Padmini. 1989. *Role of Non-Governmental Organizations and Government–NGO Relations: A Study Undertaken for the Ministry of Policy Planning and Implementation.* Colombo: Consulted at the Center for Women's Research.

Alailima, Patricia J. 1995. 'Provision of social Welfare Services', *Sri Lanka Journal of Social Sciences,* 18 (1 & 2): 1–24.

———. 1996. 'Planning and Implementation Development: Government NGO Imperatives', *Sri Lanka Journal of Social Sciences,* 19 (1 & 2): 1–26.

Appadurai, Arjun. 1996. *Modernity at Large. Cultural Dimension of Globalization.* Minneapolis, London: University of Minnesota Press.

Bastian, Sunil and **Nicola Bastian** (eds). 1997. *Assessing Participation. A Debate from South Asia.* New Delhi: Konark Publishers.

Clark, John. 1994. *Democratising Development: The Role of Voluntary Organisations.* West Hardford, CT: Kumarian.

Farrington, John, Anthony Bebbington, Kate Wellard and **David J. Lewis.** 1993. *Reluctant Partners? Non-Governmental*

Organisations, the State and Sustainable Agricultural Development. London & New York: Routledge.

Ferguson, James. 1994. The Anti-Politics Machine. 'Development', Depoliticization, and Bureaucratic Power in Lesotho. Minneapolis: University of Minnesota Press.

Fisher, Julie. 1993. Road from Rio: Sustainable Development and the Non-Governmental Movement in the Third World. Westport, CT: Praegar.

Gallardo, Joselito S., Bikki K. Randhawa and J. Orlando. 1997. A Commercial Bank's Microfinance Program. The Case of Hatton National Bank in Sri Lanka. World Bank Discussion Paper No. 369. Washington DC: World Bank.

Gill, Stephen. 1995. 'Globalization, Market Civilization, and Disciplinary Neoliberalism', Millennium: Journal of International Studies, 24(3): 399–423.

Gunatilaka, Ramani. 1997. 'Credit Based, Participatory Poverty Alleviation Strategies in Sri Lanka: What have we Learned?', Institute of Policy Studies, Poverty and Income Distribution Series No. 2. Colombo: Institute of Policy Studies.

IRED (Innovations et Reseaux pour le Development). 1991a. Development NGOs of Sri Lanka: A Directory (revised edition). Colombo: IRED.

——. 1991b. A Directory of Foreign NGOs in Sri Lanka. Colombo: IRED.

Kamal Pasha, Mustafa. 1996. 'Globalisation and Poverty in South Asia', Millennium: Journal of International Studies, 25(3): 635–56.

Lakshman, W.D. (ed.). 1997. Dilemmas of Development. Fifty Years of Economic Change in Sri Lanka. Colombo: Sri Lanka Association of Economists.

MacDonald, Laura. 1994. 'Globalising Civil Society: International NGOs in Central America', Millenium: Journal of International Studies, 23(2): 605–34.

Malena, Carmen. 1997. 'NGO Involvement in World Bank-financed Social Funds: Lessons Learned, Environment Department Papers', Participation Series 052. Washington DC: World Bank.

Nelson, Paul J. 1996. 'International Economic Environmental Policy: Transnational NGO Networks and the World Bank's Expanding Influence', Millenium: Journal of International Studies, 25(3): 605–34.

Samaraweera, Vijaya. 1996. Participation as Spiritual Duty: The Religious Roots of the New Development Orthodoxy. Paper presented at the Boundaries and Identities Conference, Edinburgh, October 1996.

——. 1997. Promoting Three Basic Freedoms. Towards Greater Freedom of Association, Assembly and Expression in Asia. A Region-wide Research and Advocacy Project, Sri Lanka. Politics, National

Security and the Vibrancy of NGOs. Colombo: Law and Society Trust.

SEEDS (Sarvodaya Economic Enterprises Development Services). n.d. Information Brochure.

SIDA. 1996. *Partnership Africa*. SIDA.

Stirrat, R.L. 1997. 'The New Orthodoxy and Old Truths: Participation, Empowerment and Other Buzz Words', in Sunil and Nicola Bastian (eds), *Assessing Participation. A Debate from South Asia*. New Delhi: Konark Publisher.

Stirrat, R.L. and **H. Henkel.** 1997. The Development Gift: The Problem of Reciprocity in the NGO World. Unpublished.

USAID. 1997. *New Partnership Initiative (NIP). Resource Guide, A Strategic Approach to Development Partnering, Vols 1 and 2*.

UNDP. n.d. *UNDP and Civil Society Organization. Building Alliance for Development*. UNDP.

Uvin, Peter. 1996. 'Scaling up the Grassroots and Scaling Down the Summit: The Relations between Third World NGOs and the UN', in Thomas G. Weiss and Leon Gordenker (eds), *NGOs, the UN, & Global Governance*. Boulder, Colorado: Lynne Reinner.

Weiss, Thomas G. and **Leon Gordenker** (eds). 1996. *NGOs, the UN, & Global Governance*. Boulder: Lynne Reinner.

Wickramasinghe, Nira. 1997. *Humanitarian Relief Organisations and Challenges to Sovereignty: The Case of Sri Lanka. RCSS Policy Studies 1*. Colombo: Regional Center for Strategic Studies.

World Bank. 1995. *Working with NGOs. A Practical Guide to Operational Collaboration between the World Bank and Non-Governmental Organizations*. Washington DC: World Bank.

———. 1996. *Staff Appraisal Report. Sri Lanka Private Sector Infrastructure Development Project, Report No. 15391-CE*. Washington DC: World Bank.

———. n.d. A Global Partnership for Development: Working with NGOs. Washington DC: World Bank.

Chapter 4

Sovereignty and Humanitarian Relief Organizations

Introduction

The war between the Sri Lankan government and the Liberation Tigers of Tamil Eelam (LTTE) has swelled the ranks of refugees and displaced people the world over. Many displaced people, Tamils, Muslims and Sinhalese, have fled Sri Lanka to escape the army and LTTE brutalities alike. The population of displaced people has fluctuated from 1.7 million to half a million at various points in the conflict which escalated into war in 1983. After Operation Riviresa and after government forces took control of Jaffna city in early December 1995, there were, according to the Ministry of Rehabilitation and Reconstruction, over one million displaced people in Sri Lanka. A majority of them are today concentrated among the extended border zone. Most are Tamil although large numbers of Sinhalese and Muslims have also been displaced.[1] The new border zones which are the result of 13 years of war between successive Sri Lankan governments and the Liberation Tigers of Tamil Eelam constitute a swathe of land between territory controlled by the Sri Lankan government and the LTTE.

These zones are overseen and administered by a number of actors: the Sri Lankan government, the Sri Lankan army, international aid agencies from the UNHCR and the International Committee of the Red Cross (ICRC), the Service Civil Enternationale Italian Relief, OXFAM and other non-governmental relief/development organizations all invited by the Sri Lankan government. These relief organizations frequently specialize in one of the five activities that are commonly understood to compose the relief discipline: food distribution, shelter, water, sanitation, and medical care.

Recent research has subjected refugees, the displaced and humanitarian relief to new lines of inquiry (Malkki, 1996: 377–404). Unlike previous studies that sought out who were the victims, where relief took place, and what had to be done, the focus has shifted to the way systems of discourse make sense of events of the recent past. Until recently the twin questions which have been posed in the media and in academic fora were whether the refugee program has been successful or not and whether their action is politicized, meaning anti-government. This line of inquiry can be illustrated in a recent study of the situation of refugees and internally displaced people in Sri Lanka which deemed the Sri Lankan relief program one of the most successful refugee relief operations in ethnic conflict situations in the world. The US Committee for Refugees in its 1991 report on 'Sri Lanka: Island of Refugees' comments: 'Humanitarian assistance to internally displaced people in Sri Lanka can fairly be described as something of model program.... Relief and to obviously varying degrees protection—for displaced people is provided by a number of different players' (Rajasingham, 1995: 10–13).

The second question of politicization is often merged with a confused understanding of sovereignty. Sovereignty is the cornerstone of international rhetoric about state independence and freedom of action and the most common response to initiatives which seek to limit a state's action in any way is that such initiatives constitute an impermissible limitation on that state's sovereignty. Jayadeva Uyangoda in a valuable contribution points out that although humanitarian assistance in Sri Lanka is praised internationally it has become the object of popular suspicion. Humanitarian non-governmental organizations that have been working in conflict areas are branded as pro-LTTE, because they have worked among the civilians in LTTE controlled areas. The ICRC, UNHCR and Médecins sans Frontières (MSF) have been particularly liable to this accusation (Uyangoda, 1995: 62–71). There is a feeling that these organizations yield a power that challenges the prerogatives of the state. This popular anti-foreign humanitarianism sentiment reflects a peculiar attachment to state sovereignty. Indeed while the world is moving from a controlling paradigm in which state sovereignty has served as an all purpose rationalization for the abuse of civilians within a state's border towards a new understanding of sovereignty infused with a greater sense of humanitarian obligation, Sri Lanka seems to be going against the current.

This essay will attempt to look at humanitarian relief organizations in times of war as new circles of power that bestow a new meaning to sovereignty. It will analyze some of the narratives about/of humanitarian relief organizations—the focus will be on the three main organizations, UNHCR, ICRC and MSF—in relation to state sovereignty. Three narratives come to mind, the first is the narrative of the international community about humanitarianism and sovereignty which legitimizes the action of the relief organizations; the second is the narrative of the humanitarian relief organizations about themselves, their autobiographies; the third is the narrative of the society they touch or the narrative of the 'other', the traces of which are available in the media. By reading each narrative against the two others, this essay hopes to evoke the tension between globalized extra-state agencies such as UNHCR, ICRC, and MSF and a nation-state that reluctantly concedes to share sovereignty.

The Legitimizing Narrative of Humanitarian Law

Humanitarian law defines the legal instruments that rule the domain in which humanitarianism is deployed and locates organizations involved in relief within clear-cut moral and legal boundaries which cannot be overstepped. In so doing it contributes to projecting transnational humanitarian relief organizations as new sovereign communities. The actions of humanitarian relief organizations, motivated by a 'cosmopolitanist morality' (Vincent, 1986) are grounded in a respect for human life and for the principles embodied in the Declaration of Human Rights. Although these organizations seek to win the consent of political authorities rather than to override them, they place humanitarian values at a higher plane than state sovereignty.

Sovereignty and Human Rights: Colliding Principles?

At least part of the difficulty in defining sovereignty lies in the fact that sovereignty traces its historical roots to sovereigns in whose hands 'absolute' spiritual and temporal power rested. The modern notion of sovereignty and the non-intervention principle may be traced back to the 1648 Westphalian Peace Accord in which belligerent countries solemnly pledged not to intervene in each other's internal matters.[2] The primordial notion of sovereignty was conceptualized around two core components of the notion of the state, namely, the territory and the population. For writers such as Bodin, Grotius, and Hobbes, sovereign statehood denoted the absolute and secular legislative power mainly within the domestic policy domain. The issues of non-intervention and external relations were secondary.[3]

There was then a shift in the focus of the sovereignty debate. Relations between the sovereign and individuals, the legitimacy of rebelling against a tyrant who broke the social contract moved away from the center of the discourse. Instead, territorial sovereignty and the state's external relations became the focus of attention. A non-intervention principle and a principle of equality of states within the international arena were conceptualized in the eighteenth century by de Vattel and Wolf. De Vattel opted for a normative approach to the analysis of inter-state relations according to which the binding nature of international law was contingent upon a priori acceptance by the state (de Vattel, 1983; Wolf, 1970).

Thus while the early sovereignty discourse emphasized the ability of a political authority to exercise effective political control over a given territory and matters taking place within this territory as well as an active part in the balance of power system, the later discourse focused on freedom from any external interference. Emmerich de Vattel's broad conception of sovereignty made sense in an international order dominated by dangerous and self-interested tyrants.

Modern discussions of sovereignty have often addressed the question of whether one can speak of 'absolute sovereignty' for states, a power above international law. Few, if any would support such a view today and the very concept of the equality of states at least implies that the sovereign rights of each state are limited by the equally sovereign rights of others.[4]

Many writers essentially equate sovereignty with independence, the fundamental authority of the state to exercise its powers without being subservient to any outside authority. One principle upon which there seems to be universal agreement is that sovereignty is an attribute of statehood and that only states can be sovereign. The classic definition of a state is found in the 1933 Montevideo Convention on Rights and Duties of States, Article I of which provides: 'The State as a person of international law should possess the following qualifications: a/ a permanent population; b/ a defined territory; c/ government; and d/ capacity to enter into relations with other states' (Hannum, 1990: 136–65).

Limits on Sovereignty: The Issue of Human Rights

The process of the centralization of sovereignty in the state which reached its climax earlier in this century is now being reversed. The deconstruction of sovereignty and the reallocation of its attributes is a key feature of the late twentieth century. The UN Charter, adopted in 1945 and the Universal Declaration of Human Rights, enacted in 1948 have come to be seen as milestones in the redefinition of sovereignty.

The conception of 'rights' as understood today in both their legal and theoretical contexts, primarily emerged much earlier in the seventeenth and eighteenth centuries as 'natural rights' and the 'rights of man' (*droits de l'homme*). Rights were seen as claims on others to a certain kind of treatment.[5] The creation of the UN marked a fundamental change concerning protection of human rights (Art. 1 [3] of the Charter and Art. 55).

On 10 December 1948, the Universal Declaration of Human Rights was passed by the UN General Assembly. It was in the Declaration that those 'basic rights' which the UN Charter had pledged to promote three years earlier were specifically named.

But within the UN discourse, the two concepts of human rights and sovereignty have been placed on a collision course. Indeed the prohibition of state-sponsored interference against an established government is based on various grounds. To some it is inherent in the general principles which define the international system such as the doctrines of sovereignty and the sovereign equality of states and of self-determination of peoples. Others have attempted to elevate non-intervention to the status of a positive, and perhaps independent fundamental right of states. Article 2 (4) of the Charter rules out the threat or use of force against the territorial integrity or political independence of a state.

During the Cold War period, the non-intervention principle and the domestic jurisdiction clause were repeatedly misused by the communist regimes to prevent external scrutiny of human rights abuses committed within their territory. The breakdown of communism and the end of the Cold War in 1989 implied that international politics—including international debate on human rights—could be freed from these ideological restraints. During the Gulf War, the Soviet Union for the first time abstained from using its veto to block the international military humanitarian intervention. In the 1990s, both the former UN Secretary General, Perez Javier de Cuellar and the UN High Commissioner for Refugees, Sadako Ogata called for an elevation of human rights to a principle of international relations, on an equal footing with the sovereignty principle (Dacyl, 1996: 139). Whether the situation is one of anarchy, acquiescence or resistance, recent international actions put states on notice that major violence against their own populations no longer will be considered exclusively a matter of domestic jurisdiction. The rights of individuals increasingly are viewed as not being matters of sovereign discretion.

Humanitarian Law Instruments

The terms 'human rights' and 'humanitarian law' are commonly used to refer to the international protection of rights and freedoms. While human rights law is applicable in peacetime, 'humanitarian law' is the law applicable during periods of armed conflict.[6] International humanitarian law can thus be defined as the principles and rules that limit the use of violence during armed conflicts. Its goals are to spare persons not directly involved in hostilities (such as those wounded and sick, shipwrecked, prisoners of war, civilians, and medical and sanitary personnel); spare the objects necessary for survival; and limit the effects of combat violence to the amount proportionally necessary for war.[7]

History

Before 1864, humanitarian problems arising from armed conflicts were generally the object of ad hoc agreements among the belligerent. Such treaties (cartels) were therefore limited in time and space. Lacking more comprehensive legal protection, war victims fared poorly.[8] At the turn of the twentieth century although an increasing number of scholars began to recognize the legality of humanitarian intervention, there were doctrinal differences due to the fact that no clear distinction was made between intervention by states to protect their citizens, humanitarian intervention, and mere intercession in favor of individuals mistreated by their own states (Dacyl, 1996: 140–41). Intervention generally describes the exercise of public authority within a foreign jurisdiction in the absence of consent of the local sovereign. In the case of 'humanitarian intervention' such activity would have the aim of assisting significant segments of a population, or a people, in circumstances of grave humanitarian emergency. Such an emergency may be the result of a natural disaster or of the inability of a government to meet the basic needs of its population effectively. What is important is that legally, only acts attributable to a state or a governmental organization can qualify as 'intervention'. If individuals or groups conduct humanitarian activities within a foreign jurisdiction, and without the consent of the local sovereign, they are according to traditional doctrine, simply in violation of local law (Griffith et al., 1995: 40).

Even today, consensus with regard to the legality of humanitarian interventions in the post-Cold War era is missing. There are of course many conventional and customary rules of international law which give the international community both the right (*droit d'ingérence humanitaire*) and the duty (*devoir d'ingérence humanitaire*) to initiate humanitarian action. The principles of humanitarian law which are already agreed upon and ratified by states are codified in the Geneva Conventions of 1949 and the Additional Protocols of 1977 that elaborate the rights and responsibilities of political authorities and humanitarian organizations. Together those six instruments of international law enumerate more than 600 provisions.

The Four 1949 Geneva Conventions

These Conventions demand respect for human beings in time of armed conflict and provide that persons not directly participating in the hostilities, such as the sick, the wounded, or prisoners shall be protected and that anyone in distress shall be helped and cared for without discrimination. Today practically all states have ratified or acceded to the Conventions, on which the ICRC work is based.

The Two 1977 Additional Protocols

Because of new practices and the evolution of armed conflicts after 1949, it became evident that the four Conventions no longer provided sufficient legal protection for all victims especially civilians. Those treaties therefore needed to be supplemented and extended by new texts. On 8 June 1977, a diplomatic conference convened in Geneva adopted two Protocols additional to the four Conventions and applicable in the event of:

a. international armed conflict.
b. non-international armed conflict.

As many analysts have noted, the conventions and protocols are not as hard a law as the domestic law of most countries that is adjudicated in the courts and backed up by specific enforcement. Humanitarian law is 'softer' and is implemented or not in the actual behavior of soldiers and government officials.

The Sri Lankan State and Humanitarian Law

Many states have not signed or ratified the treaties which govern humanitarian law. In South Asia, where non-military humanitarian intervention is often mistaken for and misconstrued as belligerent intervention, states have rarely signed all the laws relating to humanitarianism.

Sri Lanka is party to the Geneva Convention relative to the Protection of Civilian Persons in Time of War of 12 August 1949 and is therefore bound by its provisions. Article 3 of the Convention (common to the four Geneva Conventions and applicable to situations of internal armed conflict) provides for minimum standards of protection to civilians.

Sri Lanka has not, however, signed Protocol II Additional to the Geneva Conventions of 1949 relating to the victims of internal armed conflicts. The protocol develops and supplements Article 3 of the Fourth Geneva Convention. The Working Group on Enforced or Involuntary Disappearances recommended in the report of its second visit to Sri Lanka (E/CN.4/1993/25/Add.1, para 146 [d]) that the government should consider becoming a party to Protocol II Additional to the Geneva Conventions. Senior officials attributed the reluctance of the government to do so to the fear that it would imply a 'recognition' of the rebel force, despite the guarantees to the opposite provided in Article 3 of the Additional Protocol.

Sri Lanka has signed the International Covenant on Civil and Political Rights (recognizing the competence of the Human Rights Committee under Article 41 of the Covenant) and the International Covenant on Economic, Social, and Cultural Rights. It is also a party to the International Convention on the Prevention and Punishment of the Crime of Genocide, the Convention on the Rights of the Child, the Convention on the Elimination of All Forms of Discrimination against Women and other international instruments of lesser relevance to the protection of internally displaced persons.

In 1996, Sri Lanka ratified the optional protocol to the international Covenant on Civil and Political Rights. In so doing the country will be brought under a much closer and extensive scrutiny. The protocol will permit individuals to petition the Human Rights Committee on the basis that his or her right as protected by the covenant has been violated by the government of Sri Lanka. This is an unprecedented move in South Asia as only Nepal has up to now brought itself under the protocol.

However, Sri Lanka is not a party to the Convention on the non-applicability of statutory Limitations to War Crimes and Crimes against Humanity, the Convention against Torture and other Cruel, Inhuman or Degrading Treatment or Punishment, the Convention on the Reduction of Statelessness, the Convention relating to the Status of Stateless Persons and the Protocol relating to the Status of Refugees.[9]

Implementation Mechanisms

Implementation mechanisms are provided in both the 1949 Conventions and the 1977 Additional Protocols: the 171 High Contracting Parties, the ICRC, the UN, and the International Fact-Finding Commission.[10] Implementation is commonly assumed to be one of the main weaknesses in public international law. Veuthey is convinced that the essential missing ingredient in the humanitarian regime of the future is not new conventions or protocols, but greater fidelity by belligerents to existing law and more vigorous engagement by the international community.

Others indicate that it is essential, both in raising international consciousness and in ameliorating the behavior of belligerents to simplify and codify existing law so that warring parties understand their obligations and comply, particularly during civil wars.

The High Contracting Parties

According to Common Article I to the 1949 Geneva Conventions and to Additional Protocol I of 1977, states party undertake 'to respect and ensure respect for those instruments in all circumstances'. They have a double responsibility that is individual and collective. States are responsible for their own behavior (as a party to a conflict or as a neutral country), their own authorities, and for the behavior of other states party, allies or third countries.

There are a number of ways for a government to fulfil responsibilities: promoting awareness of international humanitarian law; unilaterally or multilaterally denouncing violations of international humanitarian law; supporting humanitarian organizations; preventing violations of humanitarian law in bringing political, financial, or other pressure on these parties violating the law; prosecuting violators, or at least making known publicly that these persons would be unwelcome in any capacity on their territory; and assuming the mandate of a Protecting Power. The Protecting Power, according to Article 2 of Protocol I, is a 'neutral or other State not a party to the conflict which has been designated by a party to the conflict and accepted by the adverse party and has agreed to carry out the functions assigned to a Protecting power under the Conventions and this Protocol'. Liaison among belligerents through diplomatic or other channels, the provision of relief assistance, and visits to prisoners of war and civilians are possible actions. The mechanism of the Protecting Power was used in South Asia on two occasions, in Goa in 1961 between India and Portugal; and between India and Pakistan in 1971 (Veuthey, 1993: 127–28).

The ICRC

The great merit of the ICRC founders was to have perceived the need for a single and enduring body of international law known to and applied by the states. To this end they proposed to the representatives of the governments convened in 1864 in Geneva, a text which was to become the original Geneva Convention.

The International Committee of the Red Cross (ICRC) played the central role in the codification, evolution, and dissemination of humanitarian law over a period of 125 years.

The four 1949 Geneva Conventions on the protection of war victims require ICRC delegates to pursue several tasks in all cases of international armed conflict: visit and interview prisoners of war and civilian internees; provide relief to civilians affected by armed conflict; search for missing persons and forward family messages to prisoners of war and civilian internees; offer its good offices to facilitate the institution of hospital zones and safety zones and localities; receive applications from protected persons; and undertake other humanitarian activities, subject to the consent of the parties to the conflict. According to Common Article 3 of the 1949 Geneva Conventions, in the case of an armed conflict not of an international character, the ICRC only may offer its services to the parties to the conflict. The role of ICRC is not limited to situations provided for in the Geneva Conventions, but includes any humanitarian initiative that comes within its role as a neutral and independent institution and intermediary. Governments have no obligations to accept ICRC's services in internal strife. Incentives for accepting ICRC's visits could be domestic or international. Except in cases where delegates are direct witnesses, ICRC generally pursues quiet diplomacy. Going public on violations is exceptional and remains a last resort (Veuthey, 1993: 128–30).

The International Fact-Finding Commission

The International Fact-Finding Commission, provided for in Article 90 of Protocol I was established in 1991. Any High Contracting Party to the Protocol may declare at any time that it recognizes, in relation to any other High Contracting Party accepting the same obligation, the competence of the Commission to inquire into allegations of serious violations of the Geneva Conventions and the Protocol. Only 31 states have so far accepted the competence of this Commission and they have agreed to two prerequisites for the Commission's action. The Commission is not only competent to inquire, but also to facilitate through its good offices the restoration of an attitude of respect for the Geneva Conventions and the Protocol among the parties to an armed conflict. The Commission may also conduct inquiries into serious violations, provided all the parties agree even on an ad hoc basis (ibid.: 130).

The United Nations

The United Nations as an institution has evolved substantially in its approach to humanitarian law, reasoning that laws of war were not appropriate in view of the prohibition of war in the UN Charter. The UN then sought to update its views by recognizing human rights in armed conflicts. Today the world organization regularly declares its relevance and applicability and strives to implement and enforce international humanitarian law. Since the session of the UN General Assembly after the 1968 International Conference on Human Rights in Tehran, the UN has recognized officially the value of international humanitarian law and has cooperated with the ICRC in promoting, disseminating, and implementing it.

Within the General Assembly—the world's quintessential political forum—recent discussions about the tensions between sovereignty and humanitarian access suggest a continuing evolution towards more progressive norms.

The UN Charter is based upon the principle 'of the sovereign equality of all its members' (Article 2 [1]). Given the enormous economic and political inequality of states and uncertainty about the permanence of many, it is not surprising that developing countries continue to insist upon the primacy of their sovereign rights, and regard the Charter provisions concerning human rights as essentially subsidiary. Even if there is, as some contend, an inherent contradiction in the Charter between sovereignty and human rights, few are prepared to assert a right of humanitarian intervention as inherent in the Charter.

General Assembly Resolution 46/182 (1991) steered clear of the issue. Although ambiguous in places, it does not go beyond Resolution 2816 (XXVI) (1971).[11]

The guiding principle of the new resolution states that 'the sovereignty, territorial integrity and national unity of States must be fully respected in accordance with the Charter of the United Nations' and that humanitarian assistance is to be provided with the 'consent of the affected country' thereby avoiding use of the word 'request'. Instead, assistance is to be provided in 'principle on the basis of an appeal by the affected country'.[12]

Regional Organizations

Regional organizations play an increasing role in the promotion, dissemination, and implementation of international humanitarian law. The Arab League, the Conference on Security and Cooperation in Europe, the Council of Europe, the European Parliament, the Organization of African Unity, the

Organization of American States, the Organization of the Islamic Conference have all adopted resolutions on international humanitarian law (Veuthey, 1993: 134–35).

The South Asian Association for Regional Cooperation has not taken any stands on human rights and humanitarian law. According to ICRC, human rights organizations are not pressurizing their governments to establish specifically South Asian instruments as they feel these would be something less than international standards.

International law has not resolved the tension between international civil society and the sovereign nation-state but it has provided humanitarian relief organizations with enough space to manoeuvre without contravening the two unavoidable principles of international society which are human rights and state sovereignty. Most governments today would agree with scholars who say it is unreasonable to speak of the 'absolute' sovereignty of states understood as a principle beyond or at least independent from international law. Hurst Hannum argues that sovereignty in its original sense of 'supreme' power is both 'an absurdity' and 'an impossibility' (Hannum, 1990: 15). Indeed the very concept of the equality of states implies that the sovereign rights of each state are limited by the equally sovereign rights of others. Rosenau makes an important contribution to the redefinition of sovereignty when he asserts that 'if the relative rights of states and their international communities are conceived to have political as well as legal dimensions, then the continuum between sovereignty and non-sovereignty consists of numerous values rather than just two extreme points'. He derives these values from:

- the situational determinants (the severity of the conditions within a state that evokes humanitarian concern abroad);
- the domestic determinants (the orientations of citizens and policy-makers of the state in which the humanitarian situation is located);
- the international determinants (the international milieu prevailing at the time the humanitarian situation arises); and
- the legal determinants (the legal circumstances that define the prevailing state of international law) (Rosenau, cited in Dacyl, 1996: 155–57).

Humanitarian law and human rights law have consolidated the domain of 'state sovereignty free' actors with transnational scope (Kamal Pasha, 1996). This includes UN organizations, international organizations such as the ICRC, and other non-governmental organizations that have emerged as new circles of power within the domestic society. The paradox is that while advocating that no single subject can be privileged as ethically and politically sovereign, these legal discourses in fact help create discriminate boundaries between state and non-state domains of sovereignty and new non-state sovereignties. They do not go beyond and dream a post-sovereign world.

Autobiographical Discourses: ICRC, UNHCR, and MSF

Just like nation states, political movements, and religious cults, humanitarian relief organizations are ideological/political entities. If one adopts an Aristotelian definition of the political as relating to the structure, organization, and administration of the state, humanitarian relief organizations through their action transform and are transformed by the state and society. Lefort's work helps us reflect on how these non-state organizations chart and write the 'constitution of the social space, of the form of society, of the essence of what was once termed the city'; how they evoke and justify their 'assignment of meaning to political events (*mise en sens*) and their staging in a public forum (*mise en scene*) (Lefort, 1986); how they conceptualize state sovereignty, and non-state yearnings for sovereignty; and whether they see their own roles as transcending sovereignty.

To these sort of questions scholars writing on humanitarian issues have not responded except in acknowledging that a new reality has emerged which recognizes that humanitarian action does not occur in a political vacuum. George Weiss for instance writes 'the Age of Innocence' is over for agencies and humanitarians engaged in providing assistance to afflicted peoples and argues that humanitarianism has been politicized and under certain circumstances civilian humanitarians have to temper traditional principles of neutrality and partiality (Weiss, 1995: 157–74).

This section will read the narratives or autobiographies of these three institutions and attempt to understand their ideological temperaments, political culture and conceptions of sovereignty.

Contested Identities: ICRC, MSF, and UNHCR

NGOs, IGOs, QUANGOS or Postnational Social Formations?

An anthropologist researching among refugees in Trincomalee recently voiced her exasperation concerning the confusion surrounding the term NGO. In her own words, for the average Sri Lankan in Trincomalee NGOs meant 'foreigners in four-wheel drives'.[13] This identity subsumed UN organizations, private organizations, and any individual who happened to possess a four-wheel drive vehicle. Thus the identity of humanitarian relief organizations is fuzzy as it floats somewhere there at the interface of objective and subjective definitions. Even regarding an objective definition of NGOs there is considerable confusion in both academic literature and among policy-makers.

Weiss provides us with a valuable objective definition: 'A private citizens organization, separate from government but active on social issues, not profit making, and with transnational scope' (Gordenker and Weiss, 1996: 20). If one accepts Weiss's definition, Medecins sans Frontières comes under the NGO label. But the identity of the two other relief organizations which I am focusing on clearly deviates from the accepted definitions of NGO although popular perception often coalesces all three under the same label of NGO. The International Committee of the Red Cross is often referred to as a QUANGO (quasi-non-governmental organization) by social scientists (ibib.: 21). Indeed the ICRC receives the bulk of its resources from public sources. But it can be likened to an NGO in that its services aim at internationally endorsed objectives and its operations are distinct from those of government even if its funding is public. The UNHCR is defined by scholars and practitioners both as a UN agency and, except in the perception of the people it purports to help, is rarely conflated with an NGO.

The term non-governmental organization is no longer satisfactory to qualify such complex and varied organizations. Furthermore, defining an entity negatively, by saying 'what it is not' is in itself questionable. Derrida has shown that conceptual oppositions are not simply neutral but hierarchical. One of the two terms, in this case governmental organization, is valorized and governs the other. The privileged term signifies a presence, a propriety which the other lacks.

Some scholars have suggested alternative definitions to capture the spirit of these organizations (see Chapter 1, this volume). Perhaps more significant than these objective definitions are the self-definitions of the organizations which evoke the way in which these organizations locate themselves in the world at large.

Self-definition and Autobiographies of Three Organizations

The three organizations which I chose to study were born in very different circumstances and the conditions of their birth are related in the literature they produce about themselves. In these autobiographies the self-definition and foundation are sometimes explicit and described at length, while in other cases they are eluded and cast in the realm of the non-dit. Narratives and absence of narrative provide us with some clues as to the culture of these organizations and their self-image.

The oldest institution is the ICRC. In all ICRC documents the organization is defined as a 'private independent institution'. The term NGO or even IGO is absent. A glossy ICRC information brochure unfolds the myth of origin and descent of the organization. Its origin can be traced to Solferino, a town in northern Italy, where French and Italian troops in 1859 were engaged in fierce battle against the occupying Austrian forces which was to leave 40,000 wounded and dead. The medical services of the armies were quite inadequate to cope with the situation and the wounded were abandoned to their fate. The spectacle of their suffering appalled a visiting Swiss businessman named Henry Dunant who set about helping them regardless of their nationality, calling on the local population to join him. His book entitled *A Memory of Solferino* received unexpected acclaim among Europeans, who were largely unaware of the cruel realities of war and were shocked by his description. Gustave Moynier, a lawyer who was at the time president of the Geneva Public Welfare Society immediately proposed that Dunant meet the other members of the Society to talk about his work. A five member commission was set up which adopted the name: 'International Committee for Relief to the Wounded'. During the ensuing months, the Committee's five members worked to organize an international conference which, in October 1863, brought together in Geneva the representatives of 16 states. The conference adopted a distinctive sign—a red cross on a white ground—to identify and thereby protect those who assisted wounded soldiers. It also marked the birth of the Red Cross as an institution. Subsequently the Committee took the title: 'International Committee of the Red Cross' (ICRC, n.d.).

The brochure is interesting in many respects and exemplifies the image the organization attempts to convey about itself. The vocabulary used to depict the foundation of the ICRC is nearly religious in its character: there is for instance a 'founder member' referred to in the brochure as 'the visionary who after a revelation wrote a book, reminiscent of a sacred book and decided to save humanity subsequently with the help of dedicated disciples'. Thus the ICRC seems to project the image of a religious movement or a missionary group. Its flag too reminiscent of the flags carried during the mediaeval Crusades may explain the feeling of threat felt by many people in the South when they encounter ICRC vehicles bearing the sign of the cross.

While ICRC's foundation and character are firmly rooted in the Judaeo-Christian understanding of humanitarianism and philanthropy as it existed in the nineteenth century, the UNHCR is a product of the Enlightenment. The Enlightenment project which began in the sixteenth century animated all systems of knowledge which had power in the world after the Second World War. Released from primitive superstitions and metaphysical illusions by scientific reason, the modern era was to initiate humanity's mastery of the world. Man was constructed as a reasonable and rational being and the reasonable man was the privileged center of this worldview. Reasonable man then carried on with the enlightenment project of bringing reason to the world. He constructed a system of government which ran on the principles of rational rules. The worldview of the reasonable man produced volumes of modern discourse on medicine, science, economics, sociology, politics, and the law. Modernity suggested such notions as an evolutionary conception of history, with the West showing the future of humanity (Coomaraswamy, 1994: 114–15). It also presided over the birth of international law and standards.

The birth of UNHCR which occurred nearly 75 years after that of the ICRC is closely linked to the birth of the UN and the concept of human responsibility. The brochure which relates its birth is a typical product of the rational mind: clear, to the point, factual, and informative (*UNHCR Information Paper 1994*). It conveys the idea of the inevitability of the birth of the UNHCR: there was a need for such an organization so logically the UNHCR sprang out. When the UN replaced the League of Nations in 1945, it recognized from the outset that the task of caring for refugees was a matter of international concern and that, in keeping with its Charter; the community of states should assume collective responsibility for those fleeing persecution. Accordingly, the General Assembly of the UN at its first session, held at the beginning of 1946, adopted a resolution that laid the foundation for UN activities in favor of refugees. In this resolution, the General Assembly stressed that no refugee or displaced person who had expressed valid objections to returning to his country of origin should be compelled to do so.

The UN also established a new body, the International Refugee Organization (IRO) whose mandate was to protect those refugee groups that had been recognized by the League of Nations and one new category—the 21 million or so refugees scattered throughout Europe in the aftermath of World War II. Initially the IRO's main objective was repatriation but the political build-up to the Cold War tilted the balance instead towards resettlement of those who had 'valid objections' to returning home. Such 'valid objections' included 'persecution, or fear of persecution because of race, religion, nationality or political opinions'. The IRO was replaced by the Office of the United Nations High Commissioner for Refugees (UNHCR) in 1951. While the ICRC's foundation belongs to the domain of the fictitious and the romanesque, the impression conveyed by the UNHCR self-narrative is one of tediousness and weightiness. UNHCR is a bureaucracy par excellence. Just as much as the ICRC resembles a religious movement, the foundation of the UNHCR belongs to the realm of reason, of the practical, and the logical. The concept of 'valid objection' in the matter of *refoulement* better than any other is an indication of the entrenchment of UNHCR in the values of the Enlightenment. Indeed validity suggests the ability to enunciate a reasonable judgement over the issue of *refoulement*. Thus UNHCR is grounded in a philosophico-moral tradition which goes down to the very roots of Western culture.

The birth of Medecins sans Frontières (MSF) occurred in the 1970s at a time when prodemocracy movements in countries under dictatorship were beginning to gather strength. It was also a period when young intellectuals and professionals rebelled against the prevailing system. The association was created in France in 1971—only three years after the student unrest of May 1968 – by medical doctors eager to intervene in urgent situations such as war, natural or human disasters. The organization gives little information about its founders, their names are unknown just as the exact circumstances which led to the birth of MSF (MSF, 1995). The name of Bernard Kouchner who is known to be the founder of MSF and who later as minister with the portfolio for action humanitaire argued the existence of an international right of intervention is not even mentioned. The history of MSF is a history for the present, a dehistoricized narrative.

Thus these three organizations have different styles of narrating their foundation, one mythical, the other 'reasonable', the other absent. Anthony D. Smith writing about nations and ethnic communities suggested that 'myths of origins and descent provide the means of collective location in the world and the charter of the community which explains its origins, growth and destiny' (Smith, 1993: 24). Barthes pushes the argument even further when he argues that myth is 'a depoliticized speech (parole)'. He suggests that a myth does not deny things. Rather its function is to speak about things simply. It purifies things, gives them a foundation in nature and eternity, gives them a clarity which is not that of an explanation but of the statement. The myth does not explain, it states something (Barthes, 1957).

The brochures issued by the three organizations are in a way cognitive maps of their identity and history. Born at three different periods in time, ICRC, UNHCR, and MSF construct their own social map and specific morality. Objectively, there are very few common characteristics between these three organizations except perhaps that all three were born in the North and in that sense they qualify as south-based north organizations. The ownership of the three organizations permits one to classify them as non-membership support organizations. Indeed they are not staffed and elected by the people they are meant to serve and represent. All three relief organizations are by contrast staffed by people who are socially, professionally, and, at most times, ethnically different from their clients.

It is important to assess in these three cases the internal structure of these organizations as they are narrated in the official documents in order to understand their 'culture'. By culture I mean a set of shared and enduring meanings, values, and beliefs that characterize national, ethnic, or other groups and orient their behavior. ICRC publications describe ICRC in the following way. ICRC is a private, independent institution, exclusively composed of Swiss nationals, with its headquarters in Geneva. It is neutral as regards politics, religion, and ideology. Its international character derives from its mission which is enshrined in the Geneva Conventions. The ICRC's supreme body is the Committee whose members are all Swiss citizens appointed by cooptation. The Committee's membership never exceeds 25. The Committee meets in an assembly, which sets general policies and guidelines. The institution's field operations and administration are managed by its headquarters in Geneva and by delegations set up in areas of conflict throughout the world. From this description the analogy of the religious movement can be stretched. The principle of cooptation which is common in the Catholic Church accepts the democratic idea of representation while restricting it as well to a limited congerie of candidates (*ICRC Documentation Brochure*, n.d.). In this sense the ICRC is less susceptible to adhere to the ideas of accountability or legitimacy than an organization which has a democratic structure such as the UNHCR.

The High Commissioner for Refugees is elected by the UN General Assembly on the nomination of the Secretary General. There have been eight High Commissioners since UNHCR was established in 1951. The current incumbent, Mrs Sadako Ogata (Japan) took up office on 1 January 1991. In accordance with UNHCR's Statute, the High Commissioner follows policy directives from the General Assembly and the United Nations Economic and Social Council (ECOSOC). The Executive Committee of the High Commissioner's Program (EXCOM), a body at present composed of 47 governments, oversees UNHCR budgets and advises on refugee protection. It holds an annual session in Geneva every October to approve program for the next calendar year and to set the financial target needed to implement them. It has two sub-committees: the Sub-Committee of the Whole on International Protection and the Sub-Committee on Administrative and Financial Matters. In early 1994, UNHCR employed over 4,400 persons, with some 3,500 of them in the field and the remaining 900 at headquarters. The head of the UNHCR is elected by the world representatives' meeting in the world parliament which is the General Assembly (*UNHCR Information Paper 1994*). Unlike the ICRC which reflects the ideas of the nationality which occupies its governing body, that is, the Swiss, the UNHCR attempts to convey the idea of universality by its structure and composition.

MSF consists of six independent sections (Belgium, France, Luxembourg, the Netherlands, Spain, Switzerland). MSF is an independent organization whose objective is the provision of medical and humanitarian aid for people in crisis situations. It is in this sense a private international organization. Most of its members are doctors and health workers, but many other support professions contribute to MSF's smooth functioning. In Sri Lanka, MSF Holland and MSF France are active. The example of the structure of MSF Holland worldwide can be usefully examined. The main office of MSF Holland is based in Amsterdam. On 31 December 1994, the total number of permanent and project positions at the MSF Holland office amounted to 103 and 13 respectively. Unlike the UNHCR which resembles a public sector enterprise, the structure of the MSF office is in many ways similar to that of a private sector firm. The main sections are director office, operations, control, human resources management, marketing, and communication. In 1994, 690 people were placed in MSF Holland projects. Most of them were non-medical. They belonged to 35 nationalities (MSF, 1994: 58–61).

The Charter of the Relief Organizations

What is then the role which these three organizations intend to play in the international scene? An examination of their respective charters gives some indication of the different tasks they aim to fulfil.

In 1921, the Tenth International Conference of the Red Cross adopted a resolution recognizing the ICRC as 'the guardian and promoter of the institution's fundamental moral and legal principles'. However, it was not until 1965 that the Twentieth Conference, held in Vienna, gave the movement its charter by establishing seven fundamental principles of which the ICRC was made the guardian: humanity, impartiality, neutrality, independence, voluntary service, unity, universality. The religious parallel of the Ten Commandments or the Eightfold Path is obvious here.

But apart from the charter of the ICRC, the Geneva Convention which most sovereign states have signed give this organization a special place, a place apart from other relief organizations. According to ICRC President Cornelio Sommarugga: 'Under the Geneva Convention the ICRC is responsible for protecting and assisting the victims of armed conflicts— whether international or civil—not just during the conflict itself but also following it. This is a very vast mandate, covering not only civilians who are victims of armed conflict but also those who have left their country because of those conflicts, and who are called refugees' (Refugees, 1996).

UNHCR's founding statute makes it clear that the organization's work is humanitarian and entirely non-political. It entrusts UNHCR with two main and closely related functions— to protect refugees and to promote durable solutions to their problems. According to its statute, UNHCR is competent to assist any person who 'owing to well founded fear of being persecuted for reasons of race, religion, nationality or political opinion, is outside the country of his nationality and is unable or owing to such fear or for reasons other than personal convenience, is unwilling to avail himself of the protection of that country' (General Assembly Resolution 428 [v] para 6 [1950]).

While this definition with its emphasis on individual persecution still forms the core of UNHCR's mandate, additional criteria have been progressively introduced to accommodate the evolving nature of refugee flows in recent decades. In typical situations today, UNHCR provides protection and assistance to groups of refugees fleeing combinations of prosecution, conflict, and widespread violation of human rights. In such circumstances, UNHCR usually bases its interventions on a general assessment of conditions in the refugee producing country rather than on an examination of each person's individual claim to refugee status. When UNHCR was first established, material aspects of refugee relief were seen to be the responsibility of the government which had granted asylum. However, many of world's more recent major refugee flows have occurred in LDCs. UNHCR has acquired the additional role of coordinating material assistance for refugees, returnees, and in specific instances displaced people. Although not mentioned in the organization's statute, this has become one of its principal functions alongside protection and the promotion of solutions. Initially, UNHCR's mandate was limited to people outside their country of origin. Over time, however, as part of its duty to ensure that voluntary repatriation schemes are sustainable, it has become involved in assisting and protecting returnees in their home countries. In recent years, moreover, the General Assembly and the secretary general have increasingly frequently called on UNHCR to protect or assist particular groups of internally displaced people who have not crossed an international border but are in a refugee-like situation inside their country of origin. In November 1991, for example, the secretary general asked UNHCR to assume the role of lead UN agency for humanitarian assistance to victims of the conflict in former Yugoslavia. By April 1994, it was providing massive humanitarian relief to roughly 2.8 million internally displaced persons, refugees, and other vulnerable groups in Bosnia and Herzegovina. An estimated 30 million people are internally displaced as a result of armed conflict. As civilian victims of war, they fall under the protection of international humanitarian law—specifically the

Geneva Conventions. ICRC, the guardian of those conventions works closely with UNHCR, whether in Bosnia-Herzegovina, Mozambique, Sri Lanka, Russia or the Great Lakes.

'MSF offers assistance to populations in distress, to victims of natural or man made disasters, to victims of armed conflict, without discrimination, irrespective of race, religion, creed or political affiliation. MSF observes strict neutrality and impartiality in the name of universal medical ethics and the rights to humanitarian assistance, and demands full and unhindered freedom in the exercise of its functions. MSF members undertake to respect their professional code of ethics and to observe complete independence from all political, economic or religious powers' (MSF, 1994).

The charters of these three organizations define the boundaries of their interventions and circumscribe the type of action they are able and willing to take in particular circumstances. In all three cases it involves helping the 'other' in times of war or civil conflict in order to complement the state's efforts.

Representing the 'Other'

It is common for us to see media images of refugee camps and camps for displaced people swarming with people, most often women and children with sad eyes. These people are speechless and simply gaze into the cameras while an inevitable representative of a relief organization standing in the dusty landscape in a crushed safari suit—he may belong to UNHCR, MSF or ICRC—talks with reason and concern in the name of these people and benevolently explains their plight. The purpose of my comments here is not to belittle the work performed by these organizations but to offer some insight into the way these organizations represent the people they take as objects of knowledge, assistance, and management.

An important point of entry is to look at the categories invoked by the three organizations under review. The UNHCR is concerned with 'refugees' and 'internally displaced persons' or IDPS. UNHCR documents define these categories with near technical precision. A refugee is 'a person who is outside his or her former home country owing to a well founded fear of persecution for reasons of race, religion, nationality, membership of a particular social group or political opinion, and who is unable or unwilling to avail himself or herself of the protection of that country, or to return there because of fear of persecution' (UNHCR Information Paper 1994: 5) while a displaced person is 'a person who has become a refugee but remains within his or her country'. Medecins sans Frontières is more vague. 'People in need' and 'victims' are the groups they are interested in. The ICRC focuses on 'detainees' and 'civilian population'. While the UNHCR in conformity with the Enlightenment spirit which presided to its birth draws sharp and precise boundaries around the groups they act upon, MSF remains in the realm of classical humanitarianism where the world is divided in two camps, victims and oppressors.[14] In ICRC the vocabulary is interesting as it clearly shows that its interest is in victims of violence in times of war. There are important differences in the way in which UNHCR, ICRC, and MSF represent the groups they attempt to help.

UNHCR and the Universal Refugee: The Absence of the Political

In official documents, the refugee category appears to be depoliticized while in that space an ahistorical, universal humanitarian subject is constructed. Refugees stop being specific persons and become pure victims in general: universal man, universal woman, universal child. Thus the necessary delivery of relief and long-term assistance seems to be accompanied by a host of other, unannounced social processes and practices that are dehistoricizing. The refugees become mute victims who are deemed incapable of giving credible evidence or testimony about their own condition. The plight of the refugees in UNHCR transit camps is never explained in the media by the refugees themselves. The intercessor between the refugee and the public is always a spokesperson for the UNHCR or a social worker.

Thus the humanitarian practices of the UNHCR which abstract the predicaments of displaced people from specific political, historical, cultural contexts tend to silence refugees.

ICRC and MSF: Helping Political Victims

In the case of ICRC and MSF, the elaboration of the legal refugee status into a social condition or a moral identity is quite clear. According to Mark Alther, head of the International Red Cross in Sri Lanka, there are three categories of victims. The civilian population which always suffer under war, not only in Sri Lanka, but everywhere in the whole history of the world, wounded combatants and the prisoners of war. These are the categories which are protected under the Geneva Convention (*The Sunday Leader*, 13 August 1995).

Unlike in UNHCR documents, people are not part of the universal humanity or an anonymous corporeality but are 'victims' or 'detainees' thus harboring a political identity. This difference in representation stems not only from the ideological background of these two organizations but also from the nature of the work they perform. Indeed both ICRC and MSF deal with individuals and not anonymous crowds. The very fact that ICRC collates the names of the detainees suggests that each detainee is treated as a separate person who has a separate identity. Medical doctors who treat patients in war torn zones are compelled to treat each case separately.

The individualization process does not necessarily mean that agency is given to the 'victims' or 'civilian population'. A story related to me by a medical doctor working at the Anuradhapura hospital illustrates this point. In the late morning a pregnant woman was rushed in to the Out Patients Department (OPD) by an ICRC official. He pushed though the queue of patients and demanded that his patient be taken first as it was an emergency. The woman stood behind him. As other patients began to protest the doctor came out of his room to find out what was happening and found out that the woman was seven months' pregnant and in no particular urgent condition. He asked her to join the queue. The ICRC official then raised his voice and demanded to be taken immediately. At this point the doctor quite sternly dismissed him and his patient. R. Barthes describes the victims as 'a figure for emergencies' when trying to assimilate the 'other', 'the other become a pure object, a spectacle, a clown. Relegated to the confine of humanity, he no longer threatens the security of the home' (Barthes, 1957: 152).

For ICRC and MSF there are clearly tensions when they try to locate themselves in their own discursive terms, vis-à-vis the state which embodies the old notion of sovereignty and counter-state forces that challenge and undermine that whole state-centric notional regime of sovereignty. Although the emphasis is to see victims as essentially victims of an oppressive state, in many cases the reality is more complex. In Rwanda, MSF left because it could not help and harbor those responsible for massacres. In Sri Lanka both ICRC and MSF acknowledge the fact that non-state actors too are perpetrators of violence but for them the scale of state violence outshadows the violence of others.

The concept of sovereignty does not enter the narrative of the relief organizations. 'Neutrality' is used instead to define the social space in which they perform. This social space is the boundary, the border zone, a no-man's-land, an area of conflict and tension where state and counter-state sovereignties clash. Relief organizations have constructed their role in a post-sovereign world. The concept of neutrality suggests nothing less than politics without sovereignty.

Neutrality in discursive terms may however seem to victims of non-state violence very questionable. The LTTE and the JVP, two political movements that have killed hundreds of civilians, are for instance described in the very non-committal terms of 'Tamil opposition' and 'Sinhalese opposition' (ICRC, 1994). These terms do not convey the idea that both these groups functioned at the margins of the political system in the 1980s and are in that sense quite different to the United National Party which is now the main opposition party or the TULF, the main Tamil party. Sometimes the literature produced by these organizations contain lazy inaccuracies. This can be illustrated by looking at a recent annual report of MSF. The page on Sri Lanka reads: 'Since 1983, a civil war between the Sinhalese dominated government and Tamil rebels has raged in the Island state of Sri Lanka. The Tamils make up about a quarter of the island population. Since the country's independence, in 1948, they have felt discriminated against and have been seeking to create an independent state. This eventually led to a bloody civil war....'[15]

MSF which explains the plight of the Tamils to the Tamils and to the world since most Tamils are silenced by fear of the

LTTE and by lack of opportunity to express themselves claims the production of the authoritative narrative. There is at the same time a refusal of sovereignty and a claim for a world without boundaries which in discursive terms resembles the post-structural position together with an unquestioned acceptance of 'Reason' and the values of the Enlightenment which lead to an orientalist othering process. The paradox is that these organizations which stem from and are nurtured by the rights discourse have evolved a concept of self through the practice of silencing others. While the old idea of sovereignty associated with state or nation which is taken to represent an idealized form of community is refuted in the narratives of the relief organizations, while territory and space are considered fluid entities, these postnational entities construe clear-cut boundaries between them and the 'other' victim, refugee or detainee. While sovereignty over territory is denied, sovereignty over the 'people' they act upon is consciously asserted by relief organizations.

Histories of ICRC, UNHCR, and MSF Involvement in Sri Lanka

These histories as they are related by the actors run parallel to political and social problems of the country: the JVP insurrections of 1971 and the late 1980s, and the ethnic conflict since 1983. Today the main focus of humanitarian relief is on the plight of refugees and displaced people in the northern and eastern provinces. These histories are either strangely decontextualized or they paint a moth-eaten picture of the past. The political, economic, and social problems of the country are hardly explained or if they are, they are summarized in a very definite manner.

The 1970s and the Aftermath of the JVP Insurrection

The history of ICRC in Sri Lanka is narrated in ICRC documents.[16] It commences in the 1970s when although the ICRC did not have a permanent presence in Sri Lanka it made frequent visits during the course of which it was given access to places of detention throughout the country. We learn that in

April 1971, just 20 days after the first insurrection of the Janata Vimukti Peramuna (JVP), an ICRC delegate came to Colombo and contacted the government which gave him every facility to visit hospitals where the wounded were being treated as well as places of detention.[17] The documents point to the timely intervention of the ICRC and highlights its efficiency. During these visits he saw about 1,800 persons in connection with the 5 April insurrection and arranged for the ICRC to send medical and clothing supplies for the detainees. The delegate continued visiting places of detention, seeing 5,300 detainees at the two university detention camps of Vidyalankara and Vidyodaya, and the first 'rehabilitation' camp opened at Anuradhapura hospital. This first visit lasted about six weeks. The delegate came again in September that year, by when there were 15,000 detainees in the rehabilitation camps. Reports on his visits were submitted to the authorities. The regional delegate for the Asian subcontinent continued to visit detention centers in Sri Lanka in subsequent years as ICRC annual reports reveal.

The ICRC delegate took the initiative to come to Sri Lanka in the 1970s. The government, however, extended its cooperation to the delegate. In that sense its action was a response to a particular political situation and can be qualified as a political intervention to bring assistance to victims of internal disturbances. The purpose of the visits was not to take sides in the internal conflict between the state and the JVP but to make sure that the state did not violate the rights of the detainees. Accounts of the conditions that prevail in the detention camps suggest that the ICRC visits were justified. The conditions at the temporary prison at Fort Hammenheil off the Karainagar naval base were described in these terms:

> There were in all about 150 prisoners in the Fort and the conditions in which they were kept for the first few weeks were appalling. ... The cells were so crowded that the prisoners had to lie sideways back to back in order to sleep. In a few days everybody had skin rashes caused by the heat and sweat.

A prisoner named Lamahewa died. In the inquiry which followed the Criminal Justice Commission accepted that the prisoners had been incarcerated under inhuman conditions

(Chandraprema, 1991: 40–41). The ICRC throughout the 1970s visited places of detention regularly, checking up on their lists and making sure that all those whom they have seen before remained accounted for, while registering new prisoners. This acted as a deterrent against the prisoner being done away with. The question of the guilt of the detainees, the legality or justness of the detention was not in any way part of the concern of the ICRC.

The 1980s, the Ethnic Conflict and Disappearances

During the years 1983 to 1989 the ICRC recounts how it made repeated offers to perform its humanitarian work in Sri Lanka in particular relating to assistance to the civilian population affected by the violence and visits under the emergency regulations and Prevention of Terrorism Act. These offers were made both in writing and by delegates who visited Sri Lanka to talk to the authorities. A positive response, however, came only towards the end of 1989. Finally, in October 1989, at the height of the period of JVP terror and state counter-terror, the ICRC was invited by President Premadasa to commence its humanitarian work in Sri Lanka. It was at this time able to work only in the south: the Indian Peace Keeping Force (IPKF) which was in control of the north and east did not permit the ICRC into those areas. ICRC reports lay special emphasis on the relations between the Sri Lankan state and the ICRC which presided to its entry into the country thus conveying the message that the ICRC was not comparable to any NGO but one which had an internationally recognized role.

In 1989 the ICRC renewed its offer of services to the Sri Lankan authorities, first made in 1983, to protect and assist the civilian victims of the conflict and people detained because of the events. These were the principal matters discussed with members of the government, including Mr Wijeratne, Minister for Foreign Affairs, by the ICRC delegate general for Asia and the Pacific during his mission to Colombo in May 1989. At this time the president of the ICRC received Mrs Herath, Minister for Health and Women's Affairs, at ICRC headquarters. In June, the ICRC sent a summary of its proposals to the Minister for Foreign Affairs, who again discussed them, this time with the president of the ICRC, in September in Belgrade.

During the same period, in 1987, UNHCR was established in Sri Lanka. The beginning of the current refugee crisis in Sri Lanka dates from 1983 when ethnic Tamils from the northern districts began fleeing to Tamil Nadu in southern India in large numbers. Estimates of the total number of Sri Lankan Tamil refugees in India at the height of the crisis during the period range between 165,000 and 210,000. The first large wave of refugees returned to Sri Lanka in 1987 and UNHCR responded to a request by the Government of Sri Lanka to assist in the voluntary repatriation and reintegration process.

MSF was established in Sri Lanka in 1986 when a medical and surgical unit was set up in Trincomalee. Activities were expanded to cover many conflict zones in 1987, the first mission being in Point Pedro where MSF was able to work under army protection. An MSF administrator explained that MSF did not play any role in the south during the JVP insurgency as their mandate was of a very specific nature. In the 1980s the main focus was on the peninsula.[18]

The 1990s, Disappearances, and the Problem of Displaced People

The ICRC was officially established in Sri Lanka in June 1990. Their activities included the protection of civilians in areas of conflict, escort of government supplies to rebel areas, protection of Jaffna hospital, visits to prisoners held by the LTTE, and tracing the missing. For five years the ICRC was asked by the government to escort ships to Point Pedro which is LTTE held territory. In 1995 they were asked by the government to protect food ships to Kankesanthurai. But for this they did not have security guaranties with the LTTE. The food was normally handed over to the government agent. As the ICRC had no surgical personnel in Sri Lanka, they helped the Jaffna Teaching Hospital to get medicines. The health ministry too provided aid to this hospital in the form of medicines. Ships sailing under ICRC protection enabled patients in need of special care to travel safely to Colombo for treatment and back to Jaffna. The ICRC also supported and financed the programs of the Sri Lanka Red Cross Society for displaced people in the north and east.

The resumption of the civil war in 1990 provoked a renewed exodus to Tamil Nadu. But as the situation began to stabilize, 1992 saw the beginning of a second wave of voluntary repatriation to Sri Lanka. Based on an agreement between the governments of India and Sri Lanka, the role of UNHCR was to monitor and facilitate the repatriation process. From 1992 to 1995 more than 54,000 refugees returned.

After 1987 the emphasis of UNHCR was not only on the return of refugees but also on strategies to both prevent or at least minimize the effects of involuntary displacement and also facilitate voluntary repatriation. This approach combined with a specific request in 1991 from the UN secretary general to UNHCR in Sri Lanka resulted in the extension of UNHCR assistance and to a limited extent, protection to populations (including internally displaced persons) in areas where returnees are resettling.

The volatile nature of the conflict in Sri Lanka has obliged UNHCR to take a very flexible approach in its planning and implementation. The latest phase of armed hostilities which began in April 1995 has led to significant renewed internal displacement and caused the temporary suspension of repatriation operations from India.

Its objectives in Sri Lanka covered: the protection and assistance for asylum seekers in Sri Lanka; the assistance and protection for Sri Lankan refugees returning from India; limited assistance to internally displaced persons (IDPs). Its activities included the provision of care and maintenance assistance to asylum seekers in Sri Lanka; assistance to the government in the process of voluntary repatriation of Sri Lankan refugees from India; assistance to the government in maintenance and operation of returnee transit camps in Trincomalee and Vavuniya districts and three open relief centers (ORCS) in Mannar district; provision of pre-resettlement assistance for the returnees leaving camps for their places of origin; implementation of various micro-projects to improve infrastructures in the communities receiving returnees; passive monitoring of rejected asylum seekers returned from Switzerland. UNHCR program is presently implemented in Mannar, Trincomalee, Vavuniya districts as well as Kilinochchi and Mullaitivu.

The approach taken by UNHCR is thus very much in line with the policy of the Government of Sri Lanka which encourages durable solutions for IDPs either through resettlement in places of origin or, if this is not possible in the foreseeable future, relocation in alternative sites which allow IDPs to achieve some degree of self-sufficiency. UNHCR has been the most active UN agency in the conflict zones of northeast Sri Lanka. Within the framework of 'humanitarian diplomacy' it has continually been engaged in a constructive dialogue with both the government and the LTTE on various operational issues, including assistance and protection for returnee and IDP relief program (*UNHCR Program in Sri Lanka. Information Note*, 1995).

The aims and objectives of MSF in the 1990s were to provide medical and surgical assistance in areas affected by the conflict. It was active in the following areas: Batticaloa, Madhu, Mannar, Point Pedro. Its activities included a surgical program at Point Pedro Hospital, organizing a medical program at the Madhu Open Relief Center, a surgical and obstetrical program at Mannar town (Island), at Batticaloa hospital ensuring surgical and pediatric assistance and manning in the Batticaloa district medical mobile clinics. The personnel involved were always small in number. In 1994, there were for instance in Colombo, one coordinator, one administrator, one logistician; in Madhu, one doctor, one midwife, two nurses; and in Point Pedro, one surgeon, one anaesthetist, one nurse.

MSF documents describe their other activities as the following: conveying of supply ships and trucks of the government sent to LTTE areas (114,000 metric tons in 1993); protection of the civilians in the areas of conflict; tracing the missing, family reunions, family correspondence across the lines; medical assistance to Jaffna Hospital, to mobile clinics of the Sri Lanka Red Cross Society in the north and the east to other medical structures; transfers of patients referred from Jaffna to Colombo hospitals (800 persons per year, other passengers: 2,000); dissemination of the law of war to security forces and LTTE combatants (MSF, 1994).

MSF's narrative is near technical. Its activities are neither romanticized nor overdeveloped and always described in laconic and unemotional terms as though the time was not ripe for talk but for action. Its dry narrative contrasts with that of ICRC and UNHCR which evoke in more depth their role, aims, and achievements as well as their relations with the state. The narrative of the ICRC in its annual reports and information documents concerning its intervention in Sri Lanka is particularly revealing: the non-dits are as significant as the issues privileged in their histories. What is striking are the gaps in the narrative. The reader is kept in the dark as to who the detainees are and why they have been incarcerated, why the Indian Peace Keeping Force came to Sri Lanka, what caused the refugee crisis in the 1990s. UNHCR's narrative is not one of cavities like that of ICRC but its universalizing approach tends to erase the particularities of the Sri Lankan case. One of the possible explanations is that after the end of the 1970s victims ceased to be considered in ideological terms. For many humanitarians they were no longer men, women, children or citizens who survived in the name of certain values but stomachs to be fed or bodies to be clothed. There were not good or bad deaths, only victims who deserved compassion. The UNHCR approach seems to fall in this mold. In other institutions too a change seems to have occurred. Together with humanitarian action and in conformity with its rules of neutrality and impartiality, the political has resurfaced in a more devious way. Politicization can be understood then as a more complex process, a sort of staging which relates to a mode of representation of truth. Relief organizations feel they touch upon society by shaping values, discriminating between true and false, just and unjust. This is quite clear in the difficulties they encounter to conceptualize neutrality and sovereignty. Their narratives founded on reason and neutrality point towards attempts to transcend sovereignty and the nation state and reach towards a postnational status. One may imagine them in the future as part of Derrida's vision of a new International which he described in these terms:

> ...an untimely link without status, without title, and without name, barely public even, clandestine, without coordination, without party, without country, without national community (International before, across, and beyond any national determination), without co-citizenship, without common belonging to a class (Derrida cited in Ahmad, 1996: 53).

The Other's Perception of Humanitarian Relief Narratives of the State and the Media

Although refugees, displaced persons and victims of violence are often silent objects of relief by various organizations, the latter's narrative grounded on human rights is challenged by other parties which have a voice and purport to speak in the name of the silenced. The state, mindful of its commitment to international standards and to the necessity to uphold a good international image as well as of its duty to allay the fears of certain segments of the Sinhalese community, has on many occasions spoken loud and clear through the voice of the Minister of Foreign Affairs. In civil society too various ideological blocs hostile to the human rights ideology which they perceive as a Western and dominant concept have emerged which contest both the philosophy and what they perceive as a politicized intervention of relief organizations.

Relief Organizations as Agents of Globalization

The Conspiracy Theory of Human Rights

Many Third World scholars and activists the world over adopting cultural relativist positions and denying the universality of human rights are attempting to address the question of hegemony in the human rights discourse. Many believe in what Karl Popper might describe as 'the conspiracy theory of human rights' according to which human rights are a Machiavellian creation of the West calculated to impair the economic development of the world' (Popper 1966: 94). In Sri Lanka the critique of human rights is most often linked to a critique of globalization and its main agents which are identified as foreign-funded NGOs, humanitarian relief agencies, aid agencies and the lending agencies such as the World Bank. 'Foreign-funded' organizations are commonly demonized in the Sri Lankan press. ICRC for instance receives funds through voluntary contributions, from the states party to the Geneva Conventions, from national societies, from private donors and through gifts and bequests.

With the exception of a very limited subsidy from the UN regular budget (which is used exclusively for administrative costs) UNHCR assistance programs are funded by voluntary contributions from governments, intergovernmental and non-governmental organizations, and individuals. Apart from donations by private individuals, the organization also accepts contributions from governments, international organizations, businesses, churches, and foundations.

An article in the English daily newspaper, *The Island* compared the situation in Sri Lanka where the 'subversive activity' of the NGOs was allowed to thrive with that in India:

> She (India) has thousands of NGOs but none are allowed funds from abroad for political agitation of any sort. Their human rights groups are locally funded and even they are not allowed into sensitive border areas where separatist movements exist (*The Island*, 26 November 1995).

In more sophisticated critiques from within the human rights community it is noted that human rights discourse is girded in the concepts of universalism and secularism which evolved from the European Enlightenment. Chandra Muzaffar is today one of the most virulent advocates of the notion of human dignity: 'The great challenge before us is to develop this vision of human dignity culled from our religious and spiritual philosophies into a comprehensive charter of values and principles, responsibilities and rights, and roles and relationships acceptable to human beings everywhere.' He adopts a cultural relativist position when he yearns for the need to evolve a vision of human dignity which is more just, holistic, and universal. His vision is problematic in that it is overtly theistic and homogenizing:

> In Islam, Hinduism, Sikhism, Taoism, Christianity, Judaism, and even theistic strains within Confucianism and Buddhism there are elements of such a vision of the human being, human rights and human dignity (Muzaffar, 1995: 8).

Following this line of thought human rights organizations and humanitarian relief organizations are seen as devoid of a larger spiritual and moral worldview and do not submit to God-guided values which transcend both individual and community.

It would be wrong, however, to paint a picture of Sri Lankan society as fundamentally hostile to human rights. There has been a sizable support for the NGO intervention to promote peace in the country.[19] Unlike the intervention of its opponents this movement gets little exposure in the media. Middle class based actors such as the radical intelligentsia who work in the NGO sector and the progressive human rights community adhere to Western-rational doctrines of equality but also to the individual's right to liberty and life. They see this as a necessary element of a peaceful society. A year ago thousands of peace and human rights activistes, representatives of over 40 non-party formations and non-governmental organizations staged a mass peace rally on 9 December—the eve of International Human Rights Day. The procession was accompanied by street theatre artistes who sang, danced, and portrayed the horrors of war—and the joys of peace. The crowds were kept absorbed by speeches on various themes pertaining to peace, democracy and human rights. The peace rally ended with peace torches being lit and the formal adoption of two appeals, one to the government and the other to the LTTE (*The Tamil Times*, 15 January 1995).

The Fear of Globalization

Globalization which comprises all the processes 'by which the people of the world are incorporated in a single world society' is today the site of resistance by a group of people often singled out as cultural purists who bemoan the passing of traditional values and populists fearful of an erosion of their own power bases (Baxi, 1992). The picture is, however, more complex as globalization is a multifaceted process. Those who oppose it must not be dismissed as belonging to the lunatic fringe of society. Their often excessive intervention reflects popular apprehension of being left behind while global civil society and liberalization engulf the world.[20] These manifestations of cultural protectionism are also important in that they point out to the main consequences of globalization: the rise of new social forces, the massive restructuring of international economic relations, the internationalization of the state, the emergence of novel sources and patterns of wealth and stratification on a world scale.

It is useful at this point to argue with N. Aziz building of Richard Falk's argument that there are two kinds of globalization. Globalization from above is essentially homogenizing and hegemonic. It includes political globalization which is reflected in Western countries and global financial institutions pressurizing the South to democratize. Human rights are an integral part of the process of globalization from above. In this dominant discourse, the discourse of the Western state and aid regime human rights emphasises individual and political rights to the exclusion of economic, social, and cultural rights. Globalization from below 'is represented in the form of a variety of transnational social movements that have a wide ranging concerns grounded in notion of human community that is itself based on unity in diversity' Aziz, 1995: 9–23. These movements range from environment, to women's issues, sustainable development, peace, etc. Humanitarian relief organizations are viewed by critiques as part of the process of globalization from above as they come from the North and their philosophical base is deeply embedded in the idea that reason and science can put an end to the plight of the people they attempt to help.

In Sri Lanka the intellectual critique of the modernization and globalization paradigms has, however, remained within the discourse of development in its focus on the 'development of underdevelopment'. It argues that the world's core regions create and sustain underdevelopment in the periphery of the 'third world'. This critique was also a major element in the economic nationalism of other postcolonial countries too. The argument was that Britain had caused the underdevelopment of its colonies and that left to itself it would have done much better (Van der Veer, 1994: 150). Globalization is then perceived as the history of cultural homogenization rather than as the way in which different societies appropriate the materials of modernity differently.[21]

An important feature of the anti-globalization discourse in Sri Lanka is its grounding in religion. Buddhism has been invoked to shy away the perceived threat posed by human rights and its proponents to the national culture.[22] Every constitution of the country since 1972 has stressed the special place given to Buddhism which is the religion of over 70 per cent of the population. Although Buddhism is protected by the state and practiced by the vast majority of people, many of its proponents present it as a religion under threat. Since independence, political monks organized in pressure groups take positions over crucial issues and present themselves as guides to the people by virtue of their moral prestige. When the United National Party came into power in 1977 and liberalized the economy, some monks protested against the growing consumerism. The same groups protested against the signing of the Indo-Lanka Accord of 1987 claiming that there had been a betrayal of the Sinhala people by conceding too much to the Tamils and allowing the Indians to enter the island as a peace-keeping force. The rhetoric of betrayal, and need to protect the land are ever present in the Sinhala nationalist discourse where Sinhalese and Buddhist identities are subsumed in one collapsible identity. The threat is identified as coming from the West, Christianity, and capitalism. The foreign agents are identified as belonging to the NGO sector. Little discrimination is made when speaking of NGOs. A chief monk (*mahanayake*) of the Asgiriya Chapter warned that 'some non-governmental organisations in this country who receive large amounts of foreign assistance are allegedly engaged in disrobing learned Buddhist monks and providing them secular employment' (*The Island*, 5 November 1994). This type of remark indicates a phobia vis-à-vis foreign aid and Western cultural imperialism which has spread far beyond the circles of political monks and activists.[23] What is evoked in these immediate and often emotional outbursts is the overlap between the neoliberal agenda of economic globalization and the human rights agenda of non-state actors with transnational patronage. Indeed non-state actors in Sri Lanka who strive to strengthen civil society work towards reform without upsetting or criticizing global structures. By failing to emerge as critiques of globalization they leave room for more extreme positions.

Helping the Enemy

The ICRC has been repeatedly accused in the Sinhala press of partiality towards the LTTE. The argument put forward is that the humanitarian action of the ICRC is limited to looking after the LTTE members and that its officials are not interested in securing for instance the release of soldiers of the Sri Lankan army captive in Jaffna (*Divaina*, 3 July 1993). It is less known that the army often calls upon the ICRC for help. For instance after the LTTE attack on the Puthukkudiyiruppu STF (Special task force) camp on 5 December 1995, Mr Paul Fruh, Deputy Head of ICRC in Colombo explained the duties performed by his organization: 'We were asked by the STF to take the dead LTTE combatants numbering around 60, and hand them over to the LTTE which we did while the LTTE handed over to us some 3–5 dead STF personnel which we in turn gave back to the STF' (*The Sunday Leader*, 14 January 1996).

But opponents of the ICRC stubbornly refuse to acknowledge the role this organization plays in the front and denounce its partiality towards the LTTE. This line of argument is supported by a Buddhist constituency which has as spokesperson a leading scholar *bhikku* and Kelaniya University Chancellor Venerable Walpola Rahula. The Venerable Rahula recently said about ICRC: 'This organisation here is a total fraud. It is supporting the separatist terrorists in the North. I have documents to substantiate it' (*The Daily News*, 20 July 1995). On another occasion a government controlled newspaper went so far as to describe as 'supporters of LTTE terrorists' those who asked for humanitarian concern to be shown to the displaced citizenry of the north. NGO 'traitors' were vilified and described as vultures living off the sufferings of others (*The Island*, 26 November 1995).

The critique of relief organizations does not make any distinction between local NGOs which receive foreign funds, UN organizations and international non-governmental organizations. They are all similarly condemned for intervening in a sovereign country's internal problems. The criticism levelled at the ICRC and also at MSF stems from a misunderstanding concerning their role in conflict areas. Indeed as the promoter of international humanitarian law, also known as the law of armed conflicts, the ICRC has a mandate to protect persons who are no longer participating in the hostilities. It has been mandated by the international community to monitor the application of the law of war by the parties to conflict. What some critiques fail to understand is that it is possible to pressurize a legitimate state which has signed binding treaties and conventions relating to humanitarian law but exerting similar pressure on rebel groups is hardly feasible.

What angers some strands of the public opinion is the overwhelming concern of some foreign relief organizations with the internal politics of the country. The situation varies from one organization to another. UNHCR is certainly the least 'involved' and for this reason is rarely the object of attacks in the popular press except when in March 1996 it threatened the government that it would close down its Kilinochchi operation which serves at least 100,000 people unless the government allows it to set up a standard radio communications center in that LTTE held town. MSF on the contrary has consistently taken political stands. In August 1995 for instance it signed a statement together with other humanitarian NGOs both local and foreign which appealed for a political solution to the crisis (*The Daily News*, 16 August 1995). ICRC, because it attempts to collaborate with the state and UNHCR by virtue of its statute is not part of this collective action. In circumstances such as the signing of resolutions condemning violence and appealing for peace, the issue of state sovereignty is sometimes raised in the media by detractors of NGOs, human rights activists and foreign-funded relief organizations all identified as supporters of the state's proposals for devolution of power at a regional level. In the mind of these critics, devolution paves the way for the breaking up of the sovereign nation-state and the creation of smaller sovereignties. The Ven. Walpola Rahula exemplifies this position: 'Please hold talks by all means only after defeating the LTTE.... They are now talking about a federal system.... A federal system here will signal the beginning of an Eelam state. This is a unitary state. I call upon the President to act with a sense of self-respect' (*The Daily News*, 20 July 1995). What is expressed here is in fact the fear that placed within the context of the growing power of global capital, non-state transnational actors are both acquiring the capacity to challenge the sovereignty of the state and reconstituting domestic civil society (Kamal Pasha, 1996: 646).

The Narrative of the State

The State, Conditionality, and Human Rights

The state has accepted that human rights standards represent minimum standards of justice and order that should be reflected in laws and policies within the country. In signing international covenants the state accepts that human rights are an international responsibility and that its government is accountable not only to its own citizens but also to the world community. It willingly concedes a share of its state sovereignty.

Just like most small states in the developing world, Sri Lanka is answerable to aid donor countries which take human rights in consideration when they dispense funds. It is then important that good relations are forged between the state and humanitarian relief organizations such as UNHCR or ICRC. Human rights considerations are not, however, taken into account in the context of UN development assistance. Aid is channeled in an indiscriminate way to countries governed by regimes that violate human rights. Indeed there is a clear division of tasks and responsibilities in the UN system that deal specifically with human rights (the Human Rights Commission, the General Assembly, and the Secretariat) and those that come under the broad heading of the promotion of social and economic rights. At the UN the Sri Lankan delegation has on numerous occasions to answer questions relating to the situation of refugees and displaced people. Ambassador Nihal Rodrigo pointing out to the efforts of the government to fulfil its responsibility in a conflict situation stated: 'The government will continue supplies to the displaced even in the full knowledge that a substantial portion of such supplies will be misappropriated by the Liberation Tigers of Tamil Eelam (LTTE) for its own war efforts' (*The Daily News*, 14 November 1995).

But the state speaks a double language. The relation between the state and the humanitarian relief organizations has been quite aptly summed up in the caption 'antagonistic cooperation' (Jude Fernando, 'Accountability: NGO Dilemma', *Sunday Times*, 12 March 1995). This double language is present in the state's relation with other NGOs too and as long as the state fails to acknowledge the role played by the non-governmental sector humanitarian action whether foreign or local will be looked upon with suspicion.

The State and Sovereignty

In the 1950s with the resurgence of Sinhalese nationalism, the enactment of the Official Language Act which declared Sinhala the one official language, and the emergence of the Federal Party which pressed for a Tamil homeland, national security came to be looked upon by the state not only as an inter-state problem but also as an internal issue, that of preserving and protecting the unity of the state.

State actors became oblivious to the fact that neither nationalism nor the sovereign nation-state was a natural phenomenon outside Europe. Indeed, non-European attempts to create sovereign nation-states took place in a very different context. In general, European manifestations of nationalism were products of historical contingencies in the development of a world capitalist system in early modern Europe. Non-European manifestations on the other hand came into being initially in the context of anti-colonial and anti-imperialist struggles. Different types of states emerged in these different social and historical circumstances, only a few of which conformed to the pure principles of the sovereign nation-state model. This created a conceptual problem. The discrepancy between actual nation-states and the nation-state model lead to the common phenomenon of multi-ethnic/multinational communities parading as unified nations.

For the Sri Lankan state it is today considered absolutely crucial to protect the boundaries of the state against secessionist movements thus avoiding the dilution of state sovereignty over territory and from external intervention. The state has a rigid definition of sovereignty founded on territory/land. As all nation-states it does not hesitate to use violence to defend its territory against external threats—an eventual invasion from the subcontinent—or internal threats—JVP insurrection or Tamil militancy.[24] Those who in any way seem to protect or implicitly support the enemies of the state, be they members of local NGOs or foreign based organizations are looked upon contesting state sovereignty.

Humanitarian law and the human rights discourse have provided a counter state sovereignty discourse with legitimacy and encouraged the growth of an international civil society which is gradually eroding the very foundations of the state system. The paradox is, however, that while contesting the notion of sovereignty in the state system, international law which recognizes the legitimacy of self-determination as a principle in the international system is in turn encouraging the growth of new sovereignties. Indeed as Buchanan has forcefully argued, secessionists desire not only independence from the existing state but also sovereignty for the new political unit they seek to create. The bid for secession is clearly an effort to establish sovereignty (Buchanan, 1991). The way out of this impasse may be to widen the meaning of sovereignty. As Simpson suggests to evolve a participatory self-determination which rests on the idea of protecting the collective human and democratic rights of minorities and unrepresented peoples rather than encourage claims to territorial separation or assertions of national and racial exceptionalism. Or as Rudnitsky summarises: self-determination need not necessarily imply statehood or sovereignty at all (Simpson, 1996: 35–70, 71–90).

The State and Humanitarian Relief Organizations

Even in matters dealing with relief, the nation-state articulates its own insecure narrative of being a state from times immemorial in contrast to recently created postnational formations. The state's attitude towards relief operations is conditioned by the belief that it is the prerogative of the state to provide for its people. The relief services extended by the state through its ministry of shipping, ports, rehabilitation and reconstruction consist mainly of food and shelter for the displaced. The medical needs are looked onto by the Minister of Health. But in the area of food distribution and provision of shelter there is a considerable amount of collaboration between the ministries, the government agents and for instance UNHCR and ICRC. The open relief centers (ORCs) which were designed to provide an alternative to fleeing the country for displaced persons from conflict areas and border areas were established with the agreement of both parties involved in the conflict. They are still in existence in Pesalai (Mannar island) and Madhu (Mannar mainland). After operation Riviresa and the huge displacement that followed, UNHCR immediately procured and transported to the Vanni a considerable number of badly needed relief items including 20,000 plastic sheets which give temporary shelter for some 100,000 persons, as well as kitchen ustensils. These relief items were then distributed by the UNHCR field offices in

Kilinochchi, Madhu and Jaffna in coordination with the government agents (GAs) in the areas. Furthermore the UNHCR provided storage facilities to the different GAs in the area to be used to store food and non-food items prior to distribution (*The Daily News*, 5 March 1996).

In 1995 after the LTTE broke the truce and resumed fighting the state, a constituency emerged which criticized the government's policy of allowing humanitarian assistance through the NGOs to the LTTE controlled areas because most of the aid would end up in LTTE hands. The reaction of the government has been elusive and divided on this issue. Certain groups within the government such as the Foreign Minister Lakshman Kadirgama and the Deputy Defense Minister Anurudha Ratwatte hold a firm stand criticizing any semblance of 'intervention' on the part of organizations mandated to extend only relief to refugees and displaced persons while others such as G.L. Pieris are more accommodating. By this subtle positioning, the public is confused as to the government's policy.

In fact, the government policy is expected to channel aid through the state machinery to northern refugees and displaced persons in the Jaffna peninsula. The foreign minister announced in 1995 that the government will make use of its administration in the north and the ICRC to distribute the aid material to the refugees. Following this an ICRC chartered ship, Habarana was unloading 1,500 tonnes of flour at the LTTE controlled port of Point Pedro (*The Daily News*, 14 November 1995). The ICRC has been given a special role by the state which is compelled to use its services to escort food shipments. Other NGOs are increasingly subject to strict regulations.

In early 1996, NGOs which were earlier allowed to supply pharmaceutical stocks to troubled areas were requested to send the lists of drugs they wished to supply to the Health Ministry. These lists would first be approved by the Defense Ministry Medical Board and then the Medical Supplies Division of the Health Ministry would consider if these additional stocks were necessary. The stocks would then be distributed through the normal channels of distribution of the ministry (*The Island*, 3 January 1996). By this measure the government attempted to control the supply of drugs and to a certain extent discourage others from sending drugs to the north and east thus pandering to anti-humanitarian assistance feelings.

Even in its relation with the ICRC or the UNHCR, the government on certain occasions displays its big stick. A recent event illustrates the ambiguous position of the state vis-à-vis humanitarian relief organizations and its efforts to pander to populist feelings.

The Bombing of St. Peter's Church at Navaly. The controversy started when the ICRC issued a statement condemning the alleged bombing by the air force of the Navaly Church during 'Operation Leap Forward'. The LTTE immediately seized upon the occasion to say that the Lankan forces were bombing the very places where they had asked civilians to take refuge. It was later established that the Church was still standing. Foreign Minister Lakshman Kadirgama expressed his strong dis-approval of the ICRC issuing a statement regarding the alleged bombing of St. Peter and Paul Church at Navaly. He told diplo-mats that the ICRC should have at least informed the Presi-dential Secretariat or the foreign ministry prior to issuing the statement. The head of the ICRC in Colombo explained their position:

> What we did by this press communique we stated a fact. A minimum of 65 civilians were killed. We didn't say by the air force. We said by an air strike. What exactly happened who was responsible is the business of the Commission of Inquiry. ... The definition of a holy place is the building and the garden or whatever the place in front. What happened was that bombs fell into the compound amongst the crowd. That's why so many casualties, were reported. So the church is still standing, though damaged (*The Sunday Leader*, 13 August 1995).

ICRC then issued an apology to the Foreign Ministry. The controversy did not reemerge. This episode is interesting as an example of the power games that take place in the humani-tarian sphere. The ICRC took the initiative to issue a statement as there was a possibility that civilians were being harmed but did not think it necessary to inform the Ministry of the content of its statement thus displaying its independence and even brazenness towards the government. The Ministry after finding out that in this particular occasion the ICRC seemed to have reacted without really checking all the facts turned the situation to its advantage: not only was the Ministry able to take a firm and strong attitude towards the ICRC thus belying the accusations of pandering to the wishes of the LTTE supporting NGOs and human rights organizations but it could also look magnanimous when it called upon people to recognize some of the good work performed by the ICRC.

The position of the state towards humanitarian relief organizations is one guided by the need for international approval and by the fear of appearing too soft in the eyes of anti-human rights constituencies. It betrays the difficulties which the state encounters when confronted with organizations that conceive themselves as part of a global order where state sovereignty is no longer the overarching principle. A new social space has opened up for these organizations because of the general failure of the nation-state to fulfil its obligations towards all its citizens, especially when sovereignty is interpreted in racial or ethnic terms. The social forces which condemn globalizations and its 'agents' expect the state to recapture the areas where its sovereignty is contested, thus recreating a past situation. A better option would be to reinvent the state as a site of experimentation for limited sovereignties of communities and associations.

Conclusion

The humanitarian relief organizations studied in this chapter have emerged as new circles of power by offering new meanings to the concept of sovereignty. It is indeed by positioning themselves vis-à-vis state sovereignty that they have consolidated their role in the local society. Their power that stems from a refusal to accept state sovereignty and an indifference to its sanctions is grounded or legitimized in the discourses of humanitarian law and human rights. In their vision, the morality of urgency and of action has displaced sovereignty a long time ago. MSF, ICRC, and UNHCR have been shown, however, to have different organizational structures, different cultures, and to perceive their role and domain of action differently. They are as Pascal would say '*ni Ange ni Bete*' performing their duties according to their own understanding of their mandate and own religious, moral or rational imaginings. Their increasing role in the world today is part of the process of moving to a global order in which the nation-state is undergoing a mutation and other formations for allegiance and identity are challenging its role. What they have in common is a transnational character and a desire to play a political role beyond borders.

Notes

1. See Law and Society Trust (1995). This publication is a good example of the informative and enumerative type of writing which is produced about refugees in Sri Lanka.

2. For an overview of the historical development of the notion of sovereignty, see for instance F.H. Hinsley (1986) and A. James (1986).

3. Bodin (1577), Grotius (1925). While Grotius did promote the right of the individual he may also be counted as a non-interventionist because of the deference he showed to sovereign authority and the maintenance of international order; Hobbes (1991).

4. This section is based on the excellent article by Janina W. Dacyl (1996).

5. For details on cultural relativism in the notion of human rights, see for instance Donnelly (1982), J.W. Dacyl (1996: 139).

6. Human rights law is also applicable in times of war, particularly in times of internal conflict.

7. See V.A. Leary and Suriya Wickremasinghe (1995).

8. The Treaties of 1864, 1906 and 1929 regulated the rights of wounded soldiers in the field and those wounded at sea. The rights of the civilian population were regulated by Treaties in 1907, and prisoners of war were dealt with by the Treaty of 1929.

9. See *Basic Rules of the Geneva Conventions and their Additional Protocols* (Geneva: International Committee of the Red Cross). For details on Sri Lanka see *The Geneva Conventions and the International Committee of the Red Cross: Their Relevance to Sri Lanka*, 3rd ed. (CRM doc. EO1/7/90) (Report of the Civil Rights Movement of Sri Lanka, first published 1987); Law and Society Trust, 1995: 243–47.

10. This section is based on Michel Veuthey's 'Assessing Humanitarian Law' (Veuthey, 1993: 127–35).

11. That resolution concerned 'prompt, effective and efficient response to a Government's need for assistance'. To that end a disaster relief coordinator was appointed inter alia to coordinate relief activities in response to 'a request for disaster assistance from a stricken state' and 'to assist the government of the stricken country to assess its relief and other needs'. Disasters encompassed natural and man-made situations.

12. See Michel Veuthey (1993: 130–34). Other resolutions had been adopted before resolution 46/182 which prepared the terrain for a more interventionist role for the UN. In 1988 the General Assembly adopted Resolution 43/131 which recognized the rights of civilians to international aid and the role of NGOs in emergencies. In 1990 General Assembly Resolution 45/100 reaffirmed these rights and specifically endorsed the concept of corridors of tranquillity to facilitate the work of humanitarian agencies. Following recent General Assembly debates and adding political weight to existing legal safeguards was the creation in early 1992 of a Department of Humanitarian Affairs. The major purpose of the new unit is to assure greater coordination and effectiveness of international activities. The terms of reference provided by the General Assembly, however, circumspect and carefully crafted, contain evidence of a more assertive humanitarianism. See James Ingram (1993).

13. Conversation with Ms A. Penny, social anthropologist.

14. This process of categorization can be compared to the colonial concern with censuses, gazetteers and reports written with the purpose of gaining knowledge about the 'native' in order to govern him better. See Nira Wickramasinghe (1995: 1–27).

15. Medecins sans Frontières, *Annual Report 1994*, p. 45. The first inaccuracy relates to the proportion of Tamils in Sri Lanka. The figure of 25 per cent relates to the Tamil-speaking people in the country which includes Muslims (7.4 per cent), Indian Tamils who descend mainly from the workforce which was brought by the British to work on the plantations (5.5 per cent), and the Sri Lanka Tamils (12.6 per cent). The Muslims never identified with Tamil militancy and consistently displayed a separate identity based on Islam and in the case of the Moors claimed an Arab origin. The up-country Tamils who differed from the Jaffna Tamils in many ways especially in caste, were never supportive of the Eelam movement. Coopted by the Sinhalese state, they have kept aloof from the LTTE. The second inaccuracy pertains to the moment at which the movement for the creation of a separate state occurred. The MSF report states very authoritatively that since 1948 the

Tamils have been trying to create an independent state. In fact in the mid-1950s the leading Tamil party, the Federal Party formed in 1949, put forward the demand for a federal system of government. The Bandaranaike/Chelvanayakam Pact signed in 1958 and Senanayake/Chelvanayakam Pact signed in 1965 were two significant attempts which tried to work out a form of regional autonomy as an answer to Tamil grievances. By the early 1970s this had escalated to a demand for a separate state. The emergence of the separatist trend coincided with the enactment of the first republican Constitution in 1972.

16. This section is based on the CRM Briefing No. 2 of 1995 which is compiled almost entirely from official ICRC publications.

17. For more details on the JVP insurrection see for instance A.J. Wilson (1979), Rohan Gunaratne (1990), and C.A. Chandraprema (1991).

18. Conversation with MSF administrator, January 1997.

19. In the 1970s and 1980s human rights research centers and NGOs upholding human rights values flourished. Among them were, the Nadesan Centre, the International Centre for Ethnic Studies, the Social Scientists Association, the Movement for Inter-ethnic and Racial Justice.

20. The literature on globalization is vast. See for instance, James H. Mittelman (1996) and Mike Featherstone (1990).

21. Arjun Appadurai for instance argues that globalization is a dialogue of a sort with modernity.

22. According to Sinhala-Buddhist tradition fashioned largely by the *Vamsa* literature, Sri Lanka is the *Dharmadvipa* (the island of the faith) consecrated by the Buddha himself as the land in which his teachings would flourish. The *Mahavamsa* states that on the very day of the Buddha's death, Vijaya—the founder of the Sinhala race—landed in Sri Lanka, as if to bear witness to the Buddha's prediction. The king was traditionally the protector of Buddhism and after independence the new nation-state took over this function.

23. See for instance, *Lakbima*, 31 December 1996; *Divaina*, 26 November 1995; *Divaina*, 17 October 1995; *Divaina*, 26 November 1995.

24. Anthony Giddens (1985: 121) has defined the nation-state as 'a set of institutional forms of governance maintaining an administrative monopoly over a territory with demarcated boundaries (borders), its rule being sanctioned by law and direct control of the means of internal and external violence'.

References

Ahmad Aijaz. 1996. *Lineages of the Present. Political Essays.* New Delhi: Tulika.

Aziz, Nikhil. 1995. 'The Human Rights Debate in an Era of Globalization: Hegemony of Discourse', *Bulletin of Concerned Asian Scholars*, 27(4): 9–23.

Barthes, Roland. 1957. *Mythologies.* Paris: Edition du Seuil.

Baxi, Upendra. 1992. 'Globalization: A World without Alternative?', *ICES Annual Lecture 1992.*

Bodin, Jean. 1577 (1962). *Six Livres de La Republique* (K.D. McRae ed.). Cambridge Mass: Harvard University Press.

Buchanan, Allen. 1991. *Secession. The Morality of Political Divorce from Fort Sumter to Lithuania and Quebec.* Boulder: Westview Press.

Chandraprema, C.A. 1991. *Sri Lanka. The Years of Terror. The JVP Insurrection 1987–1989.* Colombo: Lake House.

Coomaraswamy, Radhika. 1994. 'Madness, Sexuality and Crime: Reflections on Society's Margins', in Radhika Coomaraswamy and Nira Wickramasinghe (eds), *Introduction to Social Theory*, pp. 114–15. New Delhi: Konark.

Dacyl, Janina W. 1996. 'Sovereignty versus Human Rights: From Past Discourses to Contemporary Dilemmas', *Journal of Refugee Studies*, 9(2): 136–65.

Donnelly, J. 1982. 'Human Rights and Human Dignity: An Analytic Critique of Non-Western Conceptions of Human Rights', *The American Political Science Review*, 76(2): 303–17.

Featherstone, Mike (ed.). 1990. *Global Culture: Nationalism, Globalization and Modernity.* London: Sage.

Giddens, Anthony. 1985. *A Contemporary Critique of Historical Materialism, II: The Nation State and Violence.* Cambridge: Polity Press.

Gordenker, Leon and **Thomas G. Weiss.** 1996. 'Pluralizing Global Governance: Analytical Approaches and Dimensions', in Thomas G. Weiss and L. Gordenker (eds), *NGOs, the UN, and Global Governance*, p. 20. Boulder: Lynne Reinner.

Griffith, Martin, Iain Levine and **Mark Weller.** 1995. 'Sovereignty and Suffering', in John Harriss (ed.), *The Politics of Humanitarian Intervention*, p. 40. London & New York: Pinter.

Grotius, H. 1925. 'De Jure Belli ac Pacis Libri Tres', in Scott J. Brown, *The Classics of International Law.* Oxford: Clarendon.

Gunaratne, Rohan. 1990. *Sri Lanka. A Lost Revolution. The Inside Story of the JVP.* Sri Lanka: IFS.

Hannum, Hurst. 1990. *Autonomy, Sovereignty and Self Determination*. Philadelphia: University of Pennsylvania Press.

Hinsley, F.H. 1986. *Sovereignity* (2nd edn). Cambridge: Cambridge University Press.

Hobbes, Thomas. 1991. *Leviathan*. Cambridge: Cambridge University Press.

ICRC (International Committee for the Red Cross). 1994. ICRC Annual Report. Geneva: ICRC.

———. n.d. *ICRC Documentation Brochure*. ICRC.

Ingram, James. 1993. 'The Future Architecture for International Humanitarian Assistance', in Thomas G. Weiss and Larry Minear (eds), *Humanitarianism across Borders. Sustaining Civilians in Times of War*. Boulder: Lynne Rienner.

James, A. 1986. *Sovereign Statehood*. London: Allen and Unwin.

Kamal Pasha, Mustapha. 1996. 'Globalisation and Poverty in South Asia', *Millennium*, 25(3): 635–56.

Law and Society Trust. 1995. Sri Lanka: State of Human Rights 1995. Colombo: LST.

Leary, V.A. and **Suriya Wickramasinghe.** 1995. *An Introductory Guide to Human Rights Law and Humanitarian Law*. Colombo: The Nadesan Centre (2nd edn).

Lefort, Claude. 1986. *Essais sur le Politique*. Paris: Edition du Seuil.

Malkki, Liisa H. 1996. 'Speechless Emissaries: Refugees, Humanitarianism, and Dehistoricization', *Cultural Anthropology*, 11(3): 377–404.

Mittelman, James H. (ed.). 1996. *Globalization: Critical Perspective*. Boulder: Lynne Rienner.

MSF (Medecins san Frontières). 1994. *MSF Annual Report*. Amsterdam: MSF.

———. 1995. *Populations en Danger*. Rapport annuel sur les crises majeures et l'action humanitaire. Paris: La Découverte.

Muzaffar, Chandra. 1995. 'From Human Rights to Human Dignity', *Bulletin of Concerned Asian Scholars*, 27(4): 8.

Popper, Karl J. 1966. *The Open Society and its Enemies*. New Jersey: Princeton University Press.

Rajasingham, Darini. 1995. 'Homelands, Border Zones and Refugees: Facts, Fiction, Displacements', *Pravada*: 10–13.

Refugees. 1996. *Refugees*, 1(103): 28.

Rudnitsky, Vladimir. 1996. 'Self Determination in a Modern World: Conceptual Development and Practical Application', in Mortimer Sellers (ed.), *The New World Order. Sovereignty, Human Rights and the Self-Determination of Peoples*, pp. 71–90. Oxford: Berg.

Simpson, Gerry J. 1996. 'The Diffusion of Sovereignty: Self-Determination in the Post-Colonial Age', in Mortimer Sellers (ed.)

The New World Order. Sovereignty, Human Rights and the Self-Determination of Peoples, pp. 35–70. Oxford: Berg.

Smith, Anthony D. 1993. *The Ethnic Origins of Nations*. Oxford: Blackwell.

UNHCR. 1994. *UNHCR Information Paper 1994*.

van der Veer, Peter. 1994. *Religious Nationalism. Hindus and Muslims in India*. Berkeley: University of California.

Uyangoda, Jayadeva. 1995. 'NGOs, Politics and Questions of Democracy', *Thatched Patio*, 8(1–6): 62–71.

de Vattel, E. 1983. *Le Droit des Gens ou Principes de la Loi Naturelle Appliques a la Conduite et aux Affaires des Nations et des Souverains*. Geneva: Slatkine Reprints—Henry Dunant Institute.

Veuthey, Michel. 1993. 'Assessing Humanitarian Law', in Thomas G. Weiss and Larry Minear (eds), *Humanitarianism across Borders. Sustaining Civilians in Times of War*, pp. 127–35. Boulder: Lynne Reinner.

Vincent, J. 1986. *Human Rights and International Relations*. Cambridge: Cambridge University Press.

Weiss, George. 1995. 'Military–Civilian Humanitarianism: The "Age of Innocence" is Over', *International Peace Keeping*, 2(2): 157–74.

Wickramasinghe, Nira. 1995. *Ethnic Politics in Colonial Sri Lanka*. New Delhi: Vikas.

Wilson, A.J. 1979. *Politics in Sri Lanka, 1947–1979*. London: Macmillan (2nd edn).

Wolf, J.B. 1970. *Towards a European Balance of Power, 1620–1715*. Chicago: Chicago University Press.

Conclusion

In Sri Lanka, as in most postcolonial states of South Asia, traditional social norms have, since independence, coexisted with liberal democratic institutions in an uncertain, ambiguous and often paradoxical relationship. A specific kind of modernity has emerged that is still in the making. A recent feature has been the emergence and consolidation of new forces of a transnational character (such as multilateral aid agencies, international NGOs, local NGOs with international connections and humanitarian relief organizations) as new circles of power contesting and transforming the power and sovereignty of the state through various means.

The great theorists of sovereignty wrote as if the only relevant political actors were the state and the individual. This appears clearly in the famous frontispiece of Hobbes's *Leviathan* with its image of numerous subjects making up the body of the sovereign. Historically, those who evolved the theory of sovereignty were actively hostile to associations which rivaled the state, particularly the Churches, which they saw as threatening social peace through godly militancy. Stability was impossible unless competing authorities bowed to the state. The twin notions of state and sovereignty and their two corollaries—the notions of consent and treaties—dominate the conceptual setting of diplomatic relations. These notions are the anchor for discourse on changes in the international system: all changes, it is said, must flow from the consent of states—that is to say the consent of their rulers. The traditional idea of sovereignty supposed that in every state there must be a single source of unimpeachable law. The former UN secretary general whose responsibilities make him acutely aware of the sensitivities of sovereign states acknowledges that 'the centuries-old doctrine of absolute and exclusive sovereignty no longer stands, and was in fact never so absolute as it was conceived to be in theory. An intellectual requirement of our time is to rethink sovereignty' (Ghalli, 1992–93: 89–102). As the world moves from the Cold War to the post-Cold War era, sovereignty as traditionally understood is no longer sacrosanct. The age old balance between state assertions of sovereignty and international expressions of solidarity with those who suffer has begun to shift perceptibly in favor of those in need while the idea that there are 'duties beyond borders' gains more credibility (Hoffman, 1981) Sovereignty devoid of human values increasingly appears illegitimate.

The coercive features of the state, and the manner in which it has in many instances policed groups and communities that resisted its homogenizing project, has been explored in a number of studies. In the same way, a distinctive literature has emerged on the proliferation of NGOs and the 'associational revolution' that is taking place in developing countries. This book has tried to chart another course when it argues that it is not only the bureaucratic state apparatus that restricts the burgeoning of local cultures and political freedoms but also new transnational forces—sometimes referred to collectively as global civil society. In the four essays that compose this book these new circles of power have been analyzed from a southern perspective with the aim of disclosing their Janus-like character. On the one hand they provide checks and balance to an oppressive or overdeveloped state and on the other, by promoting certain values, they are in effect capturing power in the local arena by promoting a decentering of power and by attempting to create prototypes of ideal states.

At a discursive level, the new institutions have been shown to be involved in redefining security, development, governance, civil society, and state sovereignty and gradually imposing these concepts as conceptual frameworks. Thus the meanings that are assigned to these terms today dominate all fields of discussion and debate among policy-makers, administrators, public servants, and politicians. Good governance—a word rarely heard two decades ago—is today a constant in any discussion related to aid. In the same way participation and partnership are sine qua non in any development project vyinq for funding.

The question that is rarely posed except in academic circles is whether these concepts—civil society can be taken as an example—are useful analytical tools to understand Sri Lankan realities or whether they are being imposed upon societies with the purpose of depoliticizing them. Such sinister motives are often brushed away by liberal thinkers but the language of policy papers coming from these institutions tends to support this claim. The depoliticizing of society through the creation of a social sphere called civil society is not an unintended consequence but rather the most important aim of the new forces described in this book.

The associations and organizations that are defined as constituting civil society rarely engage in a reflection upon their own identity. Is there something called civil society or is it only a shibboleth? As a concept civil society means different things to different people and has undergone revisions since the works of Hegel, Marx, and de Tocqueville. Hegel in the *Philosophy of Right* wrote that it 'tears the individual from his family ties, estranges the members of the family from one another, and recognizes them as self-subsistent persons' (Hegel, 1952: 148). Gellner more recently argued that civil society was 'a cluster of institutions and associations strong enough to prevent tyranny, but which are, none the less, entered and left freely, rather than imposed by birth or sustained by awesome ritual' (Gellner, 1994: 103).

The concept of civil society appeared in Sri Lanka two decades ago when international donors began to distance themselves from state institutions perceived as ineffectual and corrupt. Civil society—generally equated with non-governmental institutions—was generally seen as having two beneficial functions for democracy. One was to perform as a counterweight to an otherwise all-powerful state. The other was to be a 'school in democracy'. The subversive character of institutions composing 'civil society' has, however, diminished rapidly with its close and uncritical association with funding organizations of liberal and neoliberal persuasion. As more and more local NGOs are coopted by transnational forces, the entire sector is perceived as an agent of globalization that offers only a semblance of a counterweight to the power of the developmental state. New democratic forms not thought out by the Post-Enlightenment social consensus of the secularized Christian world have consequently not emerged in Sri Lanka.

The most important feature of the growth of these new circles of power has been the reconstituting of a domestic civil society. At the center of this enterprise are the human rights and humanitarian law discourses that establish the primacy of the individual as opposed to the nation. As a result, new loyalties are created while older ones such as national consciousness are undermined. The new circles of power consolidate their domain through the building of institutions and networks. The growth of indigenous NGOs supportive of their aims and values bears witness to the spread of their sphere of influence. Local NGOs become a chain in what is called global civil society that is the autonomous domain of non-state activity at the global level. While international civil society is generally understood as the sum of 'interlinked civil societies' of various countries, global civil society has distinct features—the main difference being that it acknowledges new forms of transnational political activity. The new circles of power construe an alternative logic which includes 'the simultaneous acceptance of universality as a preferred world and the recognition of human capacity for its realization' (Kamal Pasha, 1996: 642). The liberal tenet of human agency is the kernel of the new circles of power and central to the constitution of a global civil society.

This book has tried to show that the growth of civil society in Sri Lanka has been completely overshadowed by the growth of new circles of power collectively referred to as global civil society. While NGOs have been privileged as their partners in the local community notwithstanding the fragmentation, competitiveness, and unrepresentative structure of this sector, no 'associative revolution' heralded by NGOs has followed except perhaps in the policy documents of certain transnational organizations. Most NGOs have limited goals and subscribe to, rather than challenge, the prevalent regime and orthodoxies. Their role in development is marginal. Collective, mass organizations such as political parties and trade unions, in spite of their loss of appeal are yet to be eclipsed by interest groups and NGOs.

This book has argued that the timid and sometimes servile civil society of Sri Lanka is being used by transnational forces as a way of transforming more efficiently domestic politics and society. It often leads to a homogenizing of political debate about alternatives to the free market. The 'grand modern fact' of the last two decades if any is not the creation within local society of a vibrant civil society but rather the emergence of these new circles of power with a rationale of their own.

References

Gellner, Ernest. 1994. *Conditions of Liberty: Civil Society and its Rivals*. London: Hamish Hamilton.

Ghalli, Boutros Boutros. 1992–93. 'Empowering the United Nations', *Foreign Affairs*, 72(5): 89–102.

Hegel, C.W.F. 1952 (1821). *Philosophy of Right*. Trans T. Knox. Oxford: OUP.

Hoffman, S. 1981. *Duties beyond Borders. On Limits and Possibilities of Ethical International Politics*. New York: Syracuse University Press.

Kamal Pasha Mustapha. 1996. 'Globalisation and Poverty in South Asia', *Millennium Journal of International Studies* (LSE), 25(3) (Winter): 635–56.

Index

About the Author

Nira Wickramasinghe is presently Senior Lecturer in the Department of History and Political Science at the University of Colombo and Senior Fellow at the International Centre for Ethnic Studies, Colombo. A historian by training, she obtained her D.Phil. from St Antony's College, University of Oxford. She has been a Fellow at the School of Public Affairs, University of Maryland and a Visiting Professor at the Ecole des Hautes Etudes en Sciences Sociales in Paris. A recipient of the World Bank Robert McNamara Fellowship, her published works include *Ethnic Politics in Colonial Sri Lanka, 1927–1947* and *Introduction to Social Theory* (co-edited), and *History Writing: New Trends and Methodologies*. Dr Wickramasinghe has also published numerous articles in edited volumes and journals.